P9-CFN-142

THE WHITE HOUSE YEARS:
Triumph and Tragedy

THE
WHITE HOUSE
YEARS

Triumph and Tragedy

OLLIE ATKINS

P♥P

A Playboy Press Book

FIRST EDITION

Playboy and Rabbit Head design are trademarks of Playboy, 919 North Michigan Avenue, Chicago, Illinois 60611 (U.S.A.), reg. U.S. Pat., marca registrada, marque déposée.

Library of Congress Cataloging in Publication Data

Atkins, Ollie, 1916-1977
    The White House years.

    1. Atkins, Ollie, 1916-1977   2. Nixon, Richard Milhous, 1913-   3. Photographers—United States—Biography. I. Title.
TR140.A82A38   770'.92'4 [B]   77-2345
ISBN 0-87223-494-0

I have known Ollie Atkins for almost twenty-five years. I first saw his photographs in the old *Saturday Evening Post* when I was a young congressman, and right away I could see that his eye and his camera lens penetrated the superficial "news value" of an event, and captured its deeper human dimension. That is why I asked Ollie to head the White House photographic office.

As a friend, he has been with us in the good times and the bad times. As a craftsman, he did more than just take pictures of events and individuals; in effect, he wrote with photographs the intimate, inside story of the Presidential years.

Richard Nixon

THE WHITE HOUSE YEARS:
Triumph and Tragedy

PART ONE

The White House Years: Triumph

January 20, 1969 / Washington, D.C.

Anybody who thinks it's easy covering an inauguration is out of his mind. And anybody who thinks of an inauguration as one single event hasn't been there.

Part of the inauguration takes place at the Capitol and the rest of it takes place at "downtown Washington." The Capitol is actually like a separate papal state, with its own police department, its own security system, and so on.

You get your passes from the Hill, and then when you're off the Capitol grounds, you're back in the United States again. It's like going from one European country to another, with visas needed each time you cross the line.

I'd been through the ordeal before, and I knew what passes to get and what not to get, and I knew what things were worth covering and what things weren't. I'd been appointed as the President's staff photographer, to take over January 20, the minute the swearing-in ceremony started.

I had arranged with old friends in the business to get a place on the elevated stand, where I could shoot the oath of office.

With various lenses I got close-ups of Richard M. Nixon, the new President, and of Vice-President Spiro Agnew. The group was very animated, with the outgoing President, Lyndon Johnson, bear-hugging the new President as if he were very happy to see him elected.

(3)

His exuberance didn't sit too well with the man Nixon defeated. Hubert Humphrey was three or four feet away watching, and he looked very crestfallen. I took shots of the outgoing Veep because I had always liked him. A very jolly man, he has always been kind to photographers, and to me particularly.

At the end of the swearing-in ceremony, the new President and his party went into the Capitol for luncheon. I gathered up my gear and took it down to my new office in the White House basement.

Since I was part of the new administration and had a temporary White House pass from the Secret Service officers, I was entitled to walk around the place almost at random.

It was almost completely deserted! Besides the White House guards, no one was on duty. The Secret Service contingent was with the new President, of course.

The guards didn't really know who I was, although some of them recognized me as an old press photographer, and nobody challenged me at all. I went down to my office, which was located almost under the President's.

The room was completely cleaned out—only a few pencils lying around. I dumped my gear and sat there a minute or two. I didn't expect anybody in because my staff was all at work.

I had already hired several men to assist me: Bob Knudsen, my second in command, Jack Kightlinger, Carl Schumacher, Buck May, John Shannon and Bill Fitz-Patrick.

John Ehrlichman had tipped me off that movers would come into the White House and take out LBJ's office equipment, television sets, ticker tapes, and all the trappings of office. They would cart them off at precisely 12:01, the minute LBJ's term expired.

With a couple of cameras on my shoulder and my pass stuck in my pocket, I walked over to the south entrance to wait for the arrival of the President.

A live television camera was already set up and its crew hanging

Candidate Nixon reaching for the outstretched hands at a political rally during the 1968 campaign.

around. When one suspicious policeman challenged me, I pulled the pass out of my pocket and showed it to him, explaining that I was the new official White House photographer covering the President's arrival.

He didn't believe me. As a matter of fact, I didn't blame him. I felt out of place myself. He got on the phone and called someone—I have no idea whom or what was said on the other end—but finally he grunted approval and let me through.

I had about half an hour to wait.

Little by little all the press photographers showed up and finally the new President and his wife arrived for the first time officially at the White House.

I went up to a little balcony, where the rest of the press wasn't allowed. There I took pictures from higher up, without getting mixed up with the other photographers. I wanted to get a shot of the whole scene rather than concentrate on a couple of close-ups of the First Family.

When the President and Mrs. Nixon finally arrived, they came in by the South Portico entrance, immediately followed by Vice-President Agnew and Mrs. Agnew.

I got lost in the White House corridors trying to get out to photograph them all coming out the north entrance on their way to the Presidential reviewing stand, but after frantically tearing around looking for the right hallways, I did make it in position just in time.

For three hours at least I stayed in the stands waiting for the parade to go by. Then the Nixon family went back into the White House, and I took a picture of them as they were going through the door.

I knew that the Nixon family was going to sit down for a short coffee break inside. It was to be an intimate family reception, and I gave a lot of thought to covering it. After working with President Nixon during his campaign, I knew that he didn't like being badgered by photographers at certain times. I figured that now would be the right time to set the trend for the future, so I didn't cover the group. However, I remained outside, within immediate summons in case President Nixon wanted me. He didn't.

The next big event to be covered was the Inaugural Ball. I decided that I'd let Bob Knudsen take on that job and left for home in McLean, Virginia at about 10:00 P.M., which wasn't bad for the first day.

The Nixons immediately after winning the 1968 election.

January 21, 1969   /   Washington, D.C.

This was the day the President was to go to his office for the first time. I didn't know whether that meant a full working day or simply a get-acquainted session in which I'd photograph him sitting in the chair, picking up a phone, or whatever.

At 7:00 A.M. the guards let me through without a murmur. The word had apparently gotten around and they all knew what I was doing.

About 8:30 or so, when Bob Knudsen came in, the first thing he said was that we should go down and get some coffee. I didn't even know where the coffeepot was, but he did. We went down into the White House mess and filled a pot up and drank it and talked.

There was no cut-and-dried schedule of the President's activities that day, so Bob went upstairs to find out from John Ehrlichman what he could. It wasn't much. We decided we'd both cover everything to make sure we didn't goof up anything the first day.

At 9:30 Jack Kightlinger arrived, followed by Buck May, the picture editor. Neither of them knew what the schedule was, either. Even my secretary, Mary Matthews, whom I'd never met before, didn't know.

When we were all there, I held a meeting in which I explained that we were going to try to get a decent working schedule that didn't demand the terrible hours that LBJ's photographer, Yoshi Okomoto, had worked.

Those people used to be in from early in the morning until late at night, sometimes not getting out until the next day.

"I know that Mr. Nixon never stays up till three in the morning," I told them. "He has more sense than that. He usually gets in bed by midnight. I've seen him walk out of some fancy parties when he was

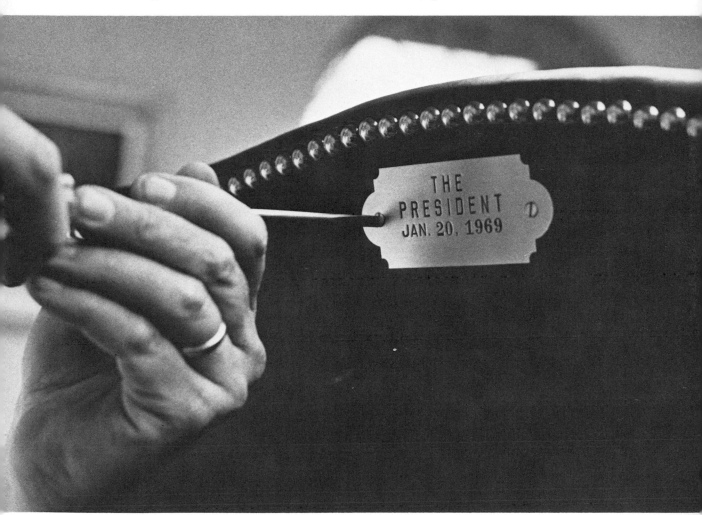

Name plate being attached to the President's chair in the Cabinet Room.

(9)

A candid shot.

Vice-President and Mrs. Eisenhower was in attendance. In fact, at ten-thirty once at Mrs. Nixon's birthday party he looked at his watch and said it was time to go home. He realized that until he went home, no one else would. So he said he was going to break the ice and he walked out. It was the greatest thing that ever happened for the working press."

I told them that for the first week we'd all be working whatever hours would be necessary until I got some idea of how the rhythm of the President's day shaped up. We'd start at nine and leave when we were through.

For the record, here's the way I was appointed official photographer for Richard M. Nixon.

I had worked for Nixon's election committee during the campaign of 1968. Actually, I was with the candidate for a little over two months, during which time he had a chance to look at me, and, of course, I had a chance to work on the campaign and to get to know everybody.

Herb Klein, chief of the Office of Communications, later told me that the President wasn't even sure he wanted an official photographer. The first official photographer to a President of the United States, Matthew Brady, had been called to the White House to take pictures of President Lincoln, Mrs. Lincoln, and little Todd.

After Brady there had been a long gap until the time of Harry Truman. There were times when the Trumans wanted pictures taken at the White House, but didn't want newsmen to do the job. They couldn't call in a commercial man because of the political implications. So instead they used a military photographer who worked for the navy and shot with a Speed Graphic. He took pictures of birthday parties—that kind of thing.

Under Eisenhower's regime, the President continued with the navy photographer and then switched to one from the army. This photographer would go along with the press and record events that took place outside the White House, getting pictures that were for the President's own personal use.

A few days after the inauguration, Nixon and Agnew visited Capitol Hill. Here Senator Everett Dirksen is offering a few words of advice.

When President Kennedy took office, he brought in Jacques Lowe as photographer. The idea was for Jacques to take all the pictures of JFK he could behind the scenes, any place he could get the President.

When President Johnson took office, there was no official White House photographer except the army and navy guys hanging around in the back room. LBJ had traveled all over the world while Vice-President, but nobody pays any attention to a Vice-President and LBJ was treated in a really shabby fashion during the Kennedy years.

A U.S. Information Agency photographer named Yoshi Okomoto had been assigned to go with the Vice-President to a NATO meeting in Belgium.

"They picked me because no one else wanted to go," Yoshi told me once. "All the other photographers hated Johnson. He was a difficult guy to work for. And no one wanted to go with the Vice-President because it was a comedown. They thought they were working for the President."

LBJ had a memory like an elephant. When he assumed the Presidency, he selected Yoshi Okomoto to be his official photographer. And LBJ told Yoshi he wanted to leave plenty of pictures of his administration to posterity.

Yoshi made thousands and thousands of pictures of the President. Every morning on the President's desk there would be stacks of 11" x 14½" prints of every frame that had been shot the day before. Johnson smiling. Johnson laughing. Johnson scowling. Johnson yawning. Sometimes the pile was two feet high.

Each morning, before tackling the problems of state, LBJ would flip through all the pictures and mark them "yes" or "no." The "yes" pictures went down to the press office and were filed in an enormous cabinet built for phonograph records. All the pictures of Johnson smiling were in one slot, all of him scowling in another, all with his feet up on the desk in still another, all with him looking out the window further on, and all with his dogs somewhere else.

This is the last photograph of Ike with President Nixon, early in 1969.

Anyone from the press could go up there and get a picture by running through the pile and selecting one.

When I took over the job, these were some of the President's first words to me:

"Ollie, how long do you think it will take you to get rid of that photographic file?"

"About sixty minutes, sir," I said.

"Do it."

In sixty minutes the file was gone.

Yoshi Okomoto's work, an excellent pictorial history of LBJ's Presidency, is now in the LBJ library.

Anyway, when Nixon was running for President, he really didn't know if he wanted to put up with the problems LBJ had in deciding about this picture or that. He figured making so many photos in the White House was needless work.

However, it was pointed out to him that he would need a photographer to do two things: make pictures of guests from time to time; and create a photographic history of his administration. On that basis, the President changed his mind and decided to select a photographer, approving me for the job.

Why me? I don't really know. He said once that he felt comfortable with me. I don't know exactly why.

Larry Higby, who worked in Bob Haldeman's office, was the one who told me I had the job. I took over on January 20.

My immediate superior was Ron Ziegler, the President's press secretary, but I don't think Ziegler really knew what to do with me. So he sort of just let me run on my own. I'm older than Ziegler and I know everybody on the press corps, having been one of them myself.

Most of them thought I was going to be a lot of help to them, but I'm afraid I wasn't able to do that much for them. That was really Ziegler's job. Anything I did was just kind of housekeeping.

February 1969 to February 1970   /   Washington, D.C.

Under President Johnson, Yoshi Okomoto had had a buzzer that would ring whenever LBJ wanted him to take a picture.

But Nixon wasn't a buzzer man. Nor did he want pictures taken all the time. So one of the first things he did was to remove the buzzer.

However, I did have an intercom speaker in my office that was hooked up to the other offices. As a result, everything that was said over the intercom in the press office was clearly audible to me. I knew immediately everything the press was told.

In addition, every time the President either arrived at or left his office somebody in the White House called me. When the caller spoke, I always had to answer, "Thank you, O.A." The idea was to give the caller my initials so he could record the fact I'd been alerted. Everyone else did the same thing. It was just a matter of keeping the records straight.

The photography office held several people. Bob Knudsen was at the back, with Mary Matthews just in front of him. Buck May came next. I was in the front with what looked like a giant-sized desk, although it wasn't really all that big.

As a matter of fact, the office was tiny. The desks and tables had been built especially small in order not to crowd the limited space. Their scaled-down size made the room look bigger.

(*17*)

President Nixon was usually a "clean desk" man. This shot of him working on briefing papers for his first European trip shows the desk as cluttered as I ever saw it.

The staff mess at the White House was operated by the navy, with navy stewards in charge of service. Only the White House staff was entitled to eat there. If you were not a member of the White House staff, you had to be invited.

No money changed hands at the mess. You signed a check each day and you were sent a bill at the end of the month.

After a week or so of using the mess and being charged for coffee and whatever, I realized I wasn't really a member. When I didn't get any invitation from anyone to join, I wrote a note to Bob Haldeman.

A couple of days later I was invited to join by Colonel Don Hughes, chief military aide to the President and head of the mess. He told me there were two classes of membership, Class I and Class II. To my surprise I discovered that I was in Class I. "Ollie, you've arrived," I told myself.

It took me a couple days to find out that Class I was actually junior membership, whereas Class II was senior membership. As a matter of practicality, Class I membership ate between 11:30 and 12:30 and Class II membership between 12:30 and 1:30. From 2:00, I think, everybody could eat there as long as the mess stayed open, and I think it usually stayed open until 3:00 if business warranted.

Well, anyway, the meals were reasonable—they cost $1.25 apiece— and they were sufficient. There were two big staff tables with Lazy Susans in the middle of them. You never knew who you were going to sit beside, and all sorts of conversations took place. If you brought a guest you had to reserve a place in advance.

It was kind of cut and dried and organized, but that's really the way the whole White House works now.

After a week or two on the job, I got into the rhythm of it. Dwight Chapin, the President's appointments secretary, kept the President's schedule. He gave Mary Matthews a copy, which she typed out on a three-by-five card and which I slipped into my coat pocket for easy reference.

Nixon in Paris. This Nixon-De Gaulle handshake broke the ice between France and the United States. Behind the President are Bob Haldeman, John Ehrlichman, Henry Kissinger, and William Rogers.

*Did you ever face so many cameras? These are American Field Service foreign
students meeting the President before returning to their homelands.*

President Nixon trying to locate the parents of a little lost boy.

I looked over the list of visitors and decided who should be photographed and who shouldn't. Then when I decided to take a picture, I went up to Dwight's office and checked with him. The idea was that sometimes the schedule got a little out of control and I might be stepping in on the wrong visitor.

I went in when Dwight indicated that it was okay. I simply opened the door and walked in. At the moment I came in, the President might be greeting his visitor, or talking to him casually, or conversing intently with him.

His favorite place to sit was on a light-colored divan. There were actually two divans facing each other in the office, next to the fireplace. He sat on the right-hand one in the farthest seat, and he liked his guest to be seated directly opposite him. A table separated the two divans; here coffee was usually served. In winter there was probably a cheery fire going in the fireplace.

On some occasions, the President paid very little attention to me. In fact, he seemed to ignore me completely. However, if he hadn't really broken the ice with his visitor yet, he used me as a kind of conversation starter.

"By the way," he'd say, "this is Ollie Atkins, my official photographer. He's going to make a couple of official photographs of us. You'll get one in the mail." And he sometimes added, "We're just doing this for the records."

When visitors were in the office who didn't really have official status, like the Easter Seal girl, or the little crippled children, he usually told me to be sure to get all the family members in the shot.

I worked faster than he expected. Lots of times he didn't realize I was through and kept waiting for me to finish. I remade a couple and then kind of nodded my head to him to let him know I was through.

When shooting, I tried to watch the President's eyes and mouth, so I wouldn't shoot when his eyes were shut or his mouth was open. When

I took a high-speed snapshot, the mouth sometimes appeared a little distorted; I tried to avoid this.

By the time the first week was out, we had thousands of requests for pictures of the President. I'm afraid I had never thought about this part of the job before taking it. Every government agency, each post office, and all kinds of institutions wanted a picture of the President to hang up.

Everyone wanted it autographed, too.

LBJ had horsed around approving and autographing individual pictures, taking hours doing so. President Nixon wasn't about to spend his time looking at pictures of himself. He decided to have several formal shots taken of him by Philippe Halsman of New York.

My job was to reproduce these as fast as possible to get them out to those who requested them. Several of the government agencies were helping out by running off two or three hundred of them at a whack for us. We had our own small laboratory, but it was overworked just getting out the daily shots of visitors and the pictures for the news services.

One of the most interesting things I observed about the President was the extent of his careful preparation for every event on his calendar. If possible, he never did anything that he wasn't completely prepared for.

Even for a minor meeting with a noncelebrity he demanded extensive briefing by means of well-researched background papers. Nixon didn't want anybody to walk in his office about whom he wasn't thoroughly briefed.

He had his staff people arrange a backgrounder ahead of time for all his meetings. After studying it carefully, he reread the material just a few seconds before the meeting actually took place.

President Nixon visiting U.S. troops in Vietnam, July 1969.

It wasn't easy getting a good picture of the President amid all the confetti during a motorcade.

This was a hot performance in Pakistan, summer of 1969. Note the air conditioner on the table next to Mrs. Nixon and food covered to keep away the flies.

Two Presidents folk dancing: the President of the United States and the President of Romania.

Another quirk was his "double" personality. I mean that he had two sides to his personality. One was his professional, business personality; the other, his family personality. He never mixed these two. In fact, a lot of businessmen I know are the same way. It doesn't make it easy to summarize such a man for the public.

There's the story, for example, about the time he was meeting one of his political aides at an airport during the campaign. The aide, quite excited, ran up to Nixon and embraced him happily, slapping him on the back exuberantly. When Mrs. Nixon, who was on the plane with the aide, came up, Nixon shook hands with her.

But that's the way he was. He just wasn't a glad-hander.

Richard Nixon was a very distant man, and even though I'd known him for some time, I really didn't feel close to him as a personal friend. I was and always would be an employee. As a matter of fact, I don't think that any of the people on the White House staff were personal friends of his, or became personal friends.

The only exception was Rose Mary Woods. She was a special, very special, staff person, the only one of the staff who was a personal friend of the Nixons—and I mean the whole family. As the President's secretary, she handled all his correspondence. She did other chores for him too, things that he trusted her with because he knew that anything he asked her to do would be done properly and with dispatch.

Even people like Herb Klein, as close as he had been to the President over the years, was still a little bit on the outside as far as a personal relationship was concerned. Of course, the President had a very special friendship with Charles G. "Bebe" Rebozo, the millionaire industrialist from Key Biscayne, Florida. But Bebe was not on the staff, so he wasn't in the same position as the rest of us.

As for the staff, it was headed up by H. R. "Bob" Haldeman. Haldeman was a very efficient and curt gentleman with whom I got along fine. He was demanding and knew that he wielded great power. As chief of staff in the White House he controlled all personnel. In addition, he was a sort of chief of staff to the President. He did everything the President asked him to do, and everything he did was done with the President's knowledge, as far as I know. There may have been rare exceptions when Haldeman did things on his own, however.

Next in line was John D. Ehrlichman, chief of domestic operations.

The best informal portrait of the President and Mrs. Nixon that I made while at the White House was taken on the covered portico outside the Oval Office.

Ehrlichman covered an entirely different area than Bob Haldeman, so if you wanted a telephone installed, it didn't do you any good to talk to John Ehrlichman. You had to get Haldeman's okay. (Haldeman's office handled most details, like the hiring and firing of people and salary adjustments and even the lists of those who could sit at the White House mess.)

And there were guys like Presidential aide Stephen Bull, Appointments Secretary Dwight Chapin, Chief of the Domestic Council Ken Cole, and a host of others. I am amazed when I think of the youth of the group. They were all such competent, hard workers and were on the run most of the time. I was very happy with the staff—happy to be part of it, even if I was older than a lot of the others. Thirty years in the business should mean something, I figured.

I heard Hubert Humphrey once say when he was Vice-President that he never could understand why there was so much jealousy between the staffs of the President and the Vice-President. He said that the two groups were at each other's throats all the time. He wondered why that should be since the President and the Vice-President weren't that way.

It was true during the Nixon administration, too. I know that most of the members of President Nixon's staff were very jealous of the President's position. They treated Vice-President Spiro Agnew rather shamefully at times. Every one knows that the Vice-President *is* the Number Two man in the country. But as a matter of fact, he's treated worse than that, as if he were a kind of a nuisance. At least that was the way it was with Nixon and Agnew.

There wasn't much good feeling between President Nixon and Vice-President Agnew. The feeling was definitely one of remoteness. From time to time President Nixon had to assign jobs to Agnew, the way a boss tells an employee what to do. But that was all there was to the association. I'm not positive about this, but I began to get the idea that this bothered Agnew very much. It wouldn't have been surprising under the circumstances.

March 1970 / Washington, D.C.

By now the President had worked out a kind of routine for himself to which he adhered pretty closely. I took notes to get it all in focus. Here's the way it went:

Every morning between 7:30 and 8:00 he got up and dressed upstairs in his quarters in the White House. Shortly after that he ate his breakfast there. The only exception was on the days when he had a guest in for breakfast. Then the two of them ate downstairs in one of the little dining rooms set up for that purpose. These "guests" were usually congressional representatives or close associates like Henry Kissinger and Alexander Haig.

My wife tells me I'm a fast eater, but I'm as slow as molasses in January compared to Richard Nixon. He simply gulped down his food. Breakfast for him lasted at most about two to three minutes.

I was informed every morning by the ushers when the President was having breakfast. I knew then that in a matter of two or three minutes he'd be on his way over to the office. Then about eight o'clock, he would actually be in the Oval Office. He might arrive at five to eight, or as late as eight-fifteen, but on the average, he got there pretty close to eight.

Although I'm only guessing, I can't see how he would have had time to visit with any members of his family before his appearance in the

The President seldom visited the press pool while traveling on Air Force One, but here he is with Ron Ziegler during a rare chat in April 1970.

office. In fact, I don't think Mrs. Nixon got up as early as he did. I'd guess that he ate by himself.

He came from his quarters to the office alone, preceded only by his valet, general handyman, and personal friend, Manolo Sanchez. (Manolo and his wife, Fina, became the Nixons' personal servants before Nixon was elected President. The President had met them and liked them when they were still working for Bebe Rebozo at Key Biscayne. After the election Manolo became the President's man, and Fina Mrs. Nixon's personal maid.)

Manolo carried the President's attaché case and anything else the President wanted him to. He walked fast to stay ahead of the President and got down to the office first to make sure everything was all right. Once inside the office he checked the fireplace and then immediately put on the coffeepot in the little pantry off to the side, so that coffee, tea, or some other beverage could be served during the President's first appointments.

At times the President didn't rush to the office. I'd see him stroll through the Rose Garden on a nice morning and admire the flowers. He'd stop and talk to the gardeners working on the flower beds, one of the rare times I ever saw him engage in small-talk. Yet on those occasions in the garden I heard him remark on how beautiful the gardens were, ask the gardeners whether everything was coming along all right, and discuss the weather in relation to the flowers.

In cold weather, the President always wore his topcoat, even for such a short walk. The minute he got to his office, Manolo helped him off with it and hung it up in the closet outside. Then the President sat down at the desk and Manolo brought him a cup of coffee.

The President spent this time of the morning looking over all the documents that had been prepared for him and had been placed on his desk by Bob Haldeman. Some of the papers were tabbed so that he could tell at a glance the priority of the subject and also whether or not it was secret.

In addition, he looked over the daily news summary at this time. This

President Nixon loved the spotlight. He came to life when he appeared in public, as at this local political rally.

meticulously prepared precis of events was the responsibility of White House staff speech writers Pat Buchanan and Ray Price. Actually, it was done by a former schoolteacher named Mort Allin, who worked with a competent staff through the night. They boiled each news item down to a couple of paragraphs and usually ended up with fifty single-spaced typewritten pages of information about domestic and foreign news. I'm not a slow reader, but I never finished reading the summary in less than twenty-five to thirty minutes. Maybe the President just skimmed through it; I don't really know. And parts of it were marked. Anyway, he usually finished it by eight-thirty.

The official day began at eight-thirty. That is when my own appointment schedule, which was a carbon copy of the President's, began. The schedule, which was always very tight, was prepared with the press in mind. An asterisk meant that once the meeting started, the press and photographers were invited in to make a picture and maybe pick up a squib of news. That was called a "press opportunity." At the proper hour, Ron Ziegler, the President's press secretary, would herd the press in, or sometimes let one of his staff do so. The press group normally consisted of somewhere between twenty to thirty-five people who would squeeze in through the door and surround the President and his guest or guests. The conference lasted for about two or three minutes, and then they would depart.

In the morning the President had certain standard appointments. One, generally the first item of business, was his visit with Bob Haldeman. The two went over all the things that were on the President's mind, and Bob faithfully wrote these down on a yellow legal pad. The yellow pad was Haldeman's Bible. Anything the President told him at one of those meetings he wrote down and acted upon as soon as possible. Right after the meeting, Bob went out to his office and relayed the President's instructions to all parts of the government and to the people on the Presidential staff.

John Ehrlichman was included in some of Haldeman's meetings with the President. Although responsible for domestic affairs, John was a little bit more than just the head of the domestic affairs branch; he was actually a close confidant of the President.

Ron Ziegler also saw Mr. Nixon every day. His job was to brief him on the situation with the press, that is, to tell him how he looked in the newspapers and on television.

No President has ever taken lightly how he is viewed by the press. For example, Lyndon Johnson knew when he was being manhandled— or when he thought he was being manhandled—and he was definitely disturbed by it. He showed it, too.

Richard M. Nixon was disturbed by what he considered unfair treatment, too. He didn't show it much, but deep down inside he didn't like it. After all, the press would never let him forget his little speech to them after he lost the California gubernatorial election: "You aren't going to have Dick Nixon to kick around anymore."

They had him around now. And guess what they were doing?

Another regular visitor to the Oval Office was Henry Kissinger, chief of the National Security Council and advisor to the President on foreign affairs. Nixon liked to deal with foreign countries through Kissinger as well as through another frequent visitor, William Rogers, the secretary of state, and the State Department representatives.

Aside from these regular meetings, the rest of the President's day was open to outside visitors.

A few details about the physical setup of the offices would be relevant here.

Rose Mary Woods was located right at his elbow, so to speak, and it was appropriate because your importance to the administration was judged by the proximity of your office to the President's Oval Office. I was the only exception to this rule. My office was really quite close to the President's—directly below it, separated only by my ceiling. And yet I was not a VIP in the Nixon hierarchy by any means.

The personnel in the West Wing were on the highest echelon. If your office was in the West Wing, even if it was down in the basement, you

This close-up of President Nixon standing in the Presidential limousine during a motorcade shows him at his vibrant best.

Motorcades were rough on cuff links, as this photograph taken in downtown New Orleans shows.

were an insider. Ron Ziegler, Rose Mary Woods, Bob Haldeman, John Ehrlichman, and Henry Kissinger were all in that sacred circle.

However, there was a kind of unpredictability about office sites. The White House was constantly being remodeled, almost on a monthly basis. Offices were redecorated, partitions taken down or put up, wallpaper changed, rugs ripped up and laid, and so on. A General Services Administration crew maintained the White House, the Executive Office Building, and any other buildings that are part of the White House. Lots of times you'd leave on Friday night and come back Monday to find old staircases down, new ones up, partitions down or up, walls changed and moved.

Nixon regarded the Oval Office as strictly a ceremonial office. I have no idea why. Other Presidents spent their office hours in the Oval Office; it was their regular working office.

Around the beginning of 1970 the GSA people went into operation one weekend and made elaborate changes in about three or four office locations right at the top of the stairs that lead from the West Executive Avenue into the Executive Office Building. The changes soon resulted in the President's EOB office—his "hideaway office," as the press dubbed it. Mr. Nixon took great pride in telling people that the real work of government was done over there.

He did most of his "homework," as he called it, in the special little hideaway office. But although he maintained that he used the White House Oval Office only as a ceremonial office, this isn't really true. He had meetings of substance in both offices. He moved from one to the other as he saw fit. I've seen him just jump up and leave the Oval Office without any notice to anyone and go over to his EOB hideaway.

To get there from the White House, he had to go outside, across a small street, and up a long stairway (at least three flights of stairs). Once there he would sit down, surrounded by thoughtful mementos and little trophies that people had given him over the years, put his feet up on a hassock, and maybe just think. Mounted on the wall of the OEB reception office were dozens of large original cartoons relating to his career.

The President didn't use the OEB office just for thinking, though. When he wanted to see a member of his staff, he summoned him or her, and the flow of traffic in and out of that office was continuous.

As everyone knows, President Nixon had two private residences in addition to the White House—one in San Clemente, California, and the other in Key Biscayne, Florida.

The San Clemente house, which was actually called La Casa Pacifica, was purchased in 1969. That's where the President meant to have his real home when he retired from the White House, and that is where he went in 1974. The house wasn't exceptionally big, but the grounds were very pleasant. It was Mrs. Nixon's favorite spot.

"Of all the places we've traveled in the world, this is the prettiest," I heard her say once. She loved to weed the beds of flowers and shrubs on the grounds. The grounds themselves were quite opulent compared to the average Southern California acreage. Cypress trees, palm trees, and eucalyptuses dotted the landscape, with the gardens laid out to accent the white-and-yellow color scheme.

The interior was furnished in French provincial style, although the President's section tended to oak and a heavy Spanish decor.

Mrs. Nixon's only complaint was that there were too few bedrooms— only five. "I like being able to entertain my husband's friends and being a hostess in my home," she said. When large groups of guests had been invited, she usually had the food catered by two local restaurants: Five Crowns and El Adobe. She once told me that the only thing she regretted not having was a silver chafing dish for official receptions.

It's hard to believe, but this lovely place, located right on the Pacific Ocean, had a railroad track running right at the bottom of the cliff between the President's residence and the beach. A train went back and forth several times a day, and so when you were going across the tracks you had to be on the lookout for it.

Adjacent to the beach was a Coast Guard loran station. (Loran—"long-range navigation"—is a radio signal device used for navigation at sea.) The station has been there since the days of World War II. When the President bought the San Clemente residence, he found it easy to install temporary buildings at the loran station. These temporary structures eventually became the one-story cluster called the Western White House, and when the President spent any time out there, all the staff members took up their duties in it.

The Western White House offices were unpretentious. In fact, the San Clemente residence, although very charming in a Spanish or Mexican way, were also relatively unpretentious, as is typical of Southern California architecture. The house did have more land around it than do most homes in California, where land is so precious and homes are generally built very close to each other.

The building itself was bigger than the normal residence for an average family, but after all the President isn't an "average" man. In fact, he had been a very successful attorney in New York before being elected to the Presidency, and his home in New York—a large and very luxurious apartment on Fifth Avenue overlooking Central Park—wasn't a normal family residence either.

Since the San Clemente place was run-down and needed repairs when he bought it, a certain amount of money was set aside to make it livable. I know a lot has been said about taxpayers' money spent on the President's private residence, but it wasn't all spent on personal things. In some cases the GSA made improvements on the grounds or in the house as part of the general housekeeping plan for the White House staff, not the Nixon family. Divans, lamps, and other things were provided for the reception areas in the office building of the Western White House. Desks, little coffee tables, and chairs for people to sit on were needed— in fact, furnishings of all kinds. This equipment belonged to the government, not to Nixon.

The Secret Service spent a good deal of money on security at the Western White House. I'm not in the security business, but I got the

President Nixon at work in his EOB hideaway office.

A close-up of the President signing a bill into law.

impression that they contrived a lot of intricate equipment that may not have been necessary. For example, there were certain electronic beams that crisscrossed the grounds so that a person walking in the area would signal his presence to the Secret Service's command post headquarters. But no one figured on the rabbits abounding there; they were continually breaking the electronic beams and setting off an alarm. Time after time a police officer or a Secret Service agent had to rush out and check to see what the disturbance was.

The White House itself was protected in the same way, but of course there aren't many rabbits in Washington. Obviously some of these electronic security devices had only been developed recently and weren't available when Eisenhower was President. When they became available, they were regarded as common security items.

If you dig up lawns and cut through the grounds to install wires and cables and set up devices, the soil has to be replaced. That costs money. The same is true about the shrubbery. But in fact, the shrubbery was used to hide the secret systems. They would put the receiving end of a beam at the end of the lawn, and then buy two or three little shrubs to plant around it to hide it. That's the reason a great deal of shrubbery was bought. I think the expenses were all legitimate. Once you give the security people the authority to secure a residence, you must let them do it right. The Secret Service makes every effort to see to it that the President is protected.

Electronic TV cameras operated by remote control surveyed the surrounding area. These cameras are very sophisticated pieces of surveillance equipment. Controlled from the command post, they could be panned around to any spot in the enclosure to take whatever picture the operator wanted. Without the protection of such detection units, it would have been quite possible for someone to slip by and do harm to the President.

I know for a fact that some people actually managed to climb over the wrought-iron fence around the White House, and that fence is over

Christmas dinner at the White House, 1970. Mamie Eisenhower joined the President, Mrs. Nixon, Tricia, and Julie and David Eisenhower.

six feet high. They walked over the White House lawn, in spite of all these signals, and approached the President's residence.

The house at Key Biscayne, also located on a beach, was bought in 1968. Actually, there were three houses there.

At Key Biscayne, the President became more a family man than a busy executive and saw more of his family than at the White House. He liked the sunshine, always preferring it to overcast weather. Once as the staff was flying to Key Biscayne, the radio predicted two days' rain in Miami.

"In that case," Nixon said to his aides, "we'll turn the plane around and head for California."

No one traveling with him knew whether or not he was kidding. But the problem was academic. The forecast was wrong, and when they got to Florida, the sun shone brightly.

Security at Key Biscayne was like that at San Clemente, even though there was less need for it because of the natural seclusion of the residence. A heliport had been built very close to the house. Although it was convenient for the President, in my own private opinion, the Secret Service overdid its construction a little bit. Instead of being out in a public area and coming to the house by means of a motorcade, the President just stepped off the helicopter, walked along the shore line, and went into his house. He was never in the public view. Great for the Secret Service.

In addition, there were shark nets dropped into the water at the little beach area in front of the residence in order to protect the President when he went in swimming. And there *were* sharks in the water. Of course the average person swimming in the Bay of Biscayne may not have a shark net, but the Secret Service regards such measures as protection for the President of the United States.

Other Presidents have had similar residences at their disposal.

Lyndon Johnson had a hangar installed at the LBJ Ranch to keep small aircraft and helicopters for flights from the Johnson ranch to the military base near Austin. They also built an airport there with runway markers and the necessary controls for landing and taking off. The hangar was air-conditioned, by the way. Can you imagine what it would cost to air-condition a hangar? In addition, the Secret Service put in various electronic devices around the Johnson ranch for security purposes and the arrival and departure of the airplanes.

I understand that the wharf where President Kennedy's yacht came in at Hyannis Port was rebuilt because it wasn't regarded as secure. All Presidents have had these things done. And certainly, much more thought has been given to security since the tragic assassination of President Kennedy. The security business has gotten bigger and bigger until now, when tight security is regarded as completely necessary. Suppose you were President and the security people were about to do all these kinds of things for you, wouldn't you just let them?

However, in view of the recent past, future Presidents may have some reservations about what should and shouldn't be done. I'm not even sure Richard Nixon himself approved the security details I've outlined; I think Bob Haldeman was the one who did. I'm not at all sure that Nixon knew about all of these electronic cameras and seeing-eye devices used for his security.

May 24, 1971   /   Key Biscayne, Florida

Shortly before David Eisenhower was about to leave for his first sea duty as an ensign in the U.S. Navy, I talked to Julie Eisenhower on an *Air Force One* flight down to Key Biscayne. I said I'd love to get some pictures of her and David at Key Biscayne before he left.

She said she would be delighted.

David wasn't in uniform yet; it was a casual time for him, his last weekend at home before going to sea.

The day I shot the pictures was a pretty busy day on which the entire press corps was down to photograph the President with Michelle Mc-Donald, the newly selected Miss United States of America. But once the press crowd had thinned out, I got Julie and David together and took them out to make the pictures.

We had decided to do a group of informal shots of the two of them fishing in the surf. Manolo Sanchez, the President's valet, scrounged up a couple of fishing rods and other gear and brought it all down to the beach in front of the house. Then he carried out two bright-colored beach chairs and set them up in the sand.

"Do you need the chairs?" Julie asked, eyeing them distastefully.

"I'm shooting color," I told her simply. "I'd like the contrast to the sand."

With Julie you could always deal straight; she's that kind of person.

She saw the point and made no further objections. After I had planted the chairs in the sand for them, Julie and David got into the swing of things, wading out into the water about fifteen feet or so. Everything was set, so I got out the walkie-talkie and signaled Jack Kightlinger to let the two wire service photographers I had promised shots to come in.

For about five minutes, AP, UPI, and Jack and I snapped all the pictures we could, showing Julie and David casting out into the surf to see what they could catch. It wasn't going to be much—the hooks weren't baited. A fish would have had to be pretty hungry to take one of those bright-colored lures. But it was a great picture session anyway, and after the films were made, I got in the car and drove back to Miami to press headquarters.

On the way a call from headquarters radio came through to me in the car. Swordfish Base (press headquarters in radio parlance) advised Hawkeye (me) that Ron Ziegler wanted to see me as soon as I got there.

"Make sure those fishing pictures don't kill off the Miss USA pictures," was what he wanted to tell me.

"How do I do that?"

"Put an embargo on the fishing pictures so they'll be for the A.M. papers only."

When I called the wire services, they agreed immediately. After all, I had set up the shots, and if it hadn't been for my special arrangement, they never would have got a piece of it. Also, they had it exclusively, with no local photographers involved. Associated Press in New York grumbled a little about accepting mandates from the White House staff, but it was just talk.

(It turned out that one of the papers I saw ran the Miss USA picture with the President, but cropped it so that Miss USA disappeared entirely and only the President showed. The same paper ran a Julie and David picture on an inside page.)

May 30, 1971 / Washington, D.C.

Returning from West Point, New York, where the President had re-
viewed the cadet pass-in-review parade the day before, we found it
raining hard in Washington. Normally I would have gone out to my
country place and spent what was supposed to have been a free Sunday
and Monday there, but because it had been raining so bad for so long
I didn't think there was much sense in mowing the grass or working in
the garden. So I stayed put with my wife and went to church on Sunday.

Sunday afternoon we were listening to the hi-fi and reading the paper
when about four o'clock I got a call from Connie Stuart, staff director
to Mrs. Nixon. She advised me that the *Time* magazine photographer
who had spent nine hours working with Tricia Nixon and Ed Cox trying to get a cover picture and color layout had done a miserable job;
at least, Tricia thought so. Could I save the situation and come up with
a photograph in color, something suitable for a cover?

To explain my feelings at that point, I'll have to backtrack to two
different picture-taking sessions, neither of which I was involved in.

The first was to celebrate in pictures the announcement of the engagement of Tricia Nixon and Ed Cox. Did they ask the White House
photographer to do the job?

No.

I'll tell you frankly, I always felt on the outside of everything that happened in the East Wing of the White House, where the family lived. The only real friend I had there was Julie Eisenhower. Julie and I enjoyed a very fine relationship. As I already said, Julie is a straight GI-type girl, someone you can speak to. She had a mind of her own, for which I respected her, and both feet planted on the ground. As a matter of fact, David, her husband, was the same way. I always worked for them, taking pictures when they wanted them. But I always acted as a professional photographer; I submitted things for their approval and listened to their comments.

With Tricia, I had never had much experience. Naturally I always got along fine with Mrs. Nixon, but Tricia had her head in the clouds and her feet way off the ground.

Ed Cox came from the big New York society crowd. There was a great built-in fear among the plebian press group, of which I am a member, that nobody in our group measured up to its standards.

Anyway, when the engagement of Tricia and Ed was announced, Tricia didn't ask us to do the photographs. She brought in a New York photographer to take shots of her and Ed after the engagement announcement. I didn't know how his arrangements were originally set up, but I did know that he was a famous photographer who had done the Grace Kelly wedding photos on an exclusive basis. Howell Conant is a very wonderful guy, and a very competent photographer, but he made the engagement pictures and had the photographs turned out by our laboratory. At first the pictures weren't pink enough. The technicians could not stand to see a color photograph coming through as pink as these appeared to be, so they made filter corrections and took some of the pink out. I think they ran off about fifty 8 x 10's, and these were submitted to the "East Side," what we called the family part, or East Wing, of the White House.

They were all turned down and sent back to me with orders to get them pinker. I called the lab. "You guys have messed it up again. You've got to make them pinker."

For technicians to make something unrealistic takes great effort, but finally they did make the prints pink enough to suit Tricia and Ed—or whoever was determining the color range—and we turned out a batch of them for the press.

When the papers got them, the technicians on the newspapers corrected them all, probably saying, "Gee, that White House lab is sure turning out lousy pink stuff." In making their engravings, they took out all the pink.

Well, somehow we survived that, but now we get up to the time when the wedding was about to take place.

Time magazine, realizing it had a good story in hand, sent over John Zimmerman, whom I had known when he was connected with the *Saturday Evening Post*. Zimmerman came to the White House under assignment by John Durniak to do a layout and cover of the couple.

John Durniak, a very serious gentleman, spent between eight and nine hours with Tricia, Ed Cox, Mrs. Nixon, and Julie. (The President wasn't involved in this at all. Nor was I, as I said. That was the day I was at West Point with him.) John Durniak went in and got everything right. He focused the camera, set it up on a tripod, put light all around in perfect positions, and checked everything out with Polaroid test shots.

The deal was that Tricia had review over the shots. That meant that what she felt was all right she would put in one pile and what she didn't in another pile. Then she could pick from what she had selected.

Well, Tricia called in Ron Ziegler and Connie Stuart and they all went over what had been made by Mr. Zimmerman. And it was disastrous.

Part of the problem was that she hadn't liked his way of working. The long arduous nine hours of photography—most of them spent waiting while the lights were adjusted and Polaroid test shots made—had set her against him.

I looked at the slides. Maybe Zimmerman hadn't had enough help. That's an important thing photographers have to think about: you have to bring enough help. I have found that if I work with very competent men like Byron Schumaker or Carl Schumacher, just the two of us working together can do almost anything.

The point is, Tricia was now facing disaster with a series of bad pictures. She had passed up the White House photography staff on two occasions, and now she was asking for help.

It didn't take me long to figure out what to do. I said I'd help if I could, then telephoned Byron Schumaker of the Interior Department who was on loan to us for the summer and asked him if he'd meet me at the office. I also had an operator call John Shannon, assistant director of our laboratory, and he got in touch with the color processor to alert him to come in to process the film.

Both loaded up with Type B Ektachrome. Byron and I arrived at the office at almost the same time. We got some lights ready, then went over to the Yellow Oval Room on the second floor of the White House. It was here that we were going to attempt to make some sort of a pleasing shot of Tricia and Ed, suitable for a *Time* magazine cover. We worked about twenty minutes with the two of them; one of us adjusted the lights, the other read the exposure, and then both of us shot when things were right.

I selected a spot I liked because we wouldn't have to move any furniture and there was a yellow curtain hanging in the background. But Tricia picked an exactly similar spot in the middle of the room. I could see at a glance that I might as well yield and not start the session off by enforcing my will on such a minor point. In order to work the setup there, we had to move a divan, a sort of elongated love seat. I grabbed one table that was in front of the piece and moved it to the side. I could see that the divan wasn't going to be so easy to move; it was, in fact, a two-man job.

"Okay, Ed," I said, "grab the other end."

Ed Cox is a towering, muscular guy, built like a basketball player. He did indeed grab one end while I grabbed the back, and we lifted it very carefully. I guess the thing weighed 250 or 300 pounds, so it was a fairly heavy item, though no piano of course. Raising it up about waist high, we started walking it out of the way. We were maneuvering it around the little tables in order to find a clear spot to put it down.

In the middle of this, Tricia suddenly looked over. "Careful," she said. "Don't forget that piece belonged to John Adams. Don't drop it."

When we began the take, it was immediately obvious that Ed and Tricia weren't going to be easy to photograph. Ed is tall, lanky. Tricia is petite. In a picture you would want Tricia's head to be just a little below Ed's, but not at his knees. You don't want the two of them to look ridiculous, so that left out the Mutt and Jeff combination for sure.

Obviously Tricia was too short standing next to her husband-to-be. I suggested Ed put one knee on a hassock to bring him down. He tried it, but he wasn't comfortable in that position. I did, however, want a shot of the two standing, so finally I cradled Tricia into Ed's left shoulder and made a portrait of both of them looking straight into the camera.

It was Fina Sanchez who suggested that we get a couple of telephone books. (The First Lady's official maid, Fina worked for the whole family too. Now, with Julie and David away, Tricia was getting the lion's share of Fina's services.) It turned out to be a great idea because that would bring Tricia's head up to the right place next to Ed. However, there were no telephone books available. Fina went tearing out of there and in a couple of minutes came back with a couple of books—I'm not sure where they came from—and Tricia stood on them next to Ed. And that's the way we made that particular picture.

I told Fina to watch Tricia's hair and if she saw even one strand out of place to rush in and brush it.

Byron was reading the light meters, and I was doing the lighting. Everybody was busy, making the most of every possible moment. Compared to the leisurely nine-hour session Tricia and Ed had had with the other photographer, I'm sure we looked like a bunch of feverishly busy bees.

We made about a half-dozen different setups so that we would have a selection to pick from. After we had both shot a roll apiece, I figured the job was done. We thanked Tricia and Ed for their cooperation and they left.

In the lab we started to shoot a test roll, running it first in the chemicals to see whether it came out all right; if it did, we'd put in the film of Tricia and Ed.

No sooner had we arranged a setup in which I was the stand-in than Tricia appeared in the doorway again. "I'd like to make another shot in the Lincoln Reading Room," she said. "Can you do that?"

"Sure," I said. "Let's go."

We stopped everything and moved our lights down to the Lincoln Room. There we made a couple of supposedly "informal" shots of Tricia and Ed having coffee, talking, and reading the paper. When we had finished these shots, we thanked them kindly and prepared to move our gear.

Tricia spoke up. "How about the Rose Garden? Can you make some pictures in the Rose Garden?"

It was a very rainy weekend. An overcast sky normally gives a blue haze to all color pictures. Besides, the grass was wet, and it was already six o'clock. Nothing could have been less conducive to good color photography.

But we said yes anyway. We had to change to daylight color material. We told them the change would take a couple of minutes, but after that we would meet them downstairs at the bottom of the elevator and go over with them.

We ran down to the photo office, removed the Type B film we'd been using and put in the daylight color stock—high-speed Ektachrome rated at 160. Then Byron with a long lens and I with a short lens went over to the bottom of the elevator just in time to meet Tricia and Ed coming down.

We went into the garden and made a half roll each of two situations.

One was on the steps where Tricia and Ed were going to be married. (These steps lead from the President's office area to the Rose Garden.) The other was actually on the grass in the Rose Garden. After we finished, we went back up to the Yellow Oval Room, finally made our test roll, broke down all the lighting and equipment, and returned to the office.

All told, we had spent about thirty-five minutes working with Tricia and Ed. Now I needed someone from the laboratory to work on the film and get it ready for Tricia to see in the morning. I telephoned Frank Vincent, the chief color technician at the lab, at his home. He was puddling cement and couldn't leave it right then.

"Finish up and come on in."

He agreed to, and as soon as he had completed the job on his patio, he changed clothes, came down to the office, picked up the film, and spent all night processing it. At 9:00 A.M. he had it in my office all ready to be examined.

The screening was held at 9:30. Present were Connie Stuart, Ron Ziegler, Paul Fisher, the White House projectionist, Helen Smith, assistant to Connie Stuart and in charge of public relations, Tricia, Carl Schumacher, my assistant, and I.

For a screening like this I use an editing projector. You can slip different shots in, change them easily, and they don't have to be in a big tray. I simply flip one slide in at a time.

We went through all the shots and Tricia was delighted with the whole take. Nothing could have made me happier, not only because I had sort of saved the day but also because I really hadn't done too much with Tricia before.

I had always had a suspicion that Tricia felt practically anybody could do a better photography job than Atkins. But here was visual proof that I could measure up to the highest-paid New York photographers.

I was honestly delighted that Tricia was so pleased and went home that night with a very warm feeling that a good job had been done.

It worked out that about half of the pictures in the *Time* layout and the cover shot came from our cameras; the rest came from the *Time* magazine photographers' cameras. All in all, Tricia got a good pre-wedding story, and it was a harmonious solution to the whole problem.

A quiet moment at Camp David.

June 7, 1971 / San Clemente, California

One of my main photographic problems with President Nixon was to get him to appear casual and to show him at ease with people around him. We had been after Ron Ziegler to get the Chief Executive to take a walk on the beach near the Western White House at San Clemente for months. Finally, on June 7, the President said he'd take a stroll for us and show us just how casual he really was. A group of us went down to set up our cameras and photograph him walking along the sand.

He came down from his residence on a switchback wooden stairway built into the steep bank. He was wearing what he considered casual clothes: shoes and socks and long trousers; a light-blue sport shirt under a Camp David jacket—a dark blue windbreaker jacket with a big Presidential seal on the front. He looked like the chairman of the board out for a walk in between acquisitions. For the record, that's about as casual as Richard M. Nixon ever got.

He went walking along the beach at the point where the waves stop, where the sand is the firmest. It's a hazardous place for walking because from time to time a wave unexpectedly comes up farther than the others. And sure enough, just about the time he got within camera range, one of those bigger waves came along and he was suddenly up to his ankles in water. He did a little dance trying to get out of the surf as we snapped our pictures.

Part One / Triumph

Oh, no! I said to myself. *They'll say he's trying to walk on the water!* But nobody picked it up. Nor did anyone wonder why he walked on the beach in shoes rather than barefoot.

Richard Nixon at the wheel of the Columbia *off Newport, California. That's sailing expert "Bus" Mosbacher in the hat.*

President and Mrs. Nixon strolling along the beach in front of their San Clemente residence.

September 25, 1971 / Kalipell, Montana

Dedication ceremonies are almost always stiff and staid affairs. There is a rostrum, and various politicians say their piece and then someone makes a symbolic gesture to start whatever machinery there is running. Then the power goes on, or the dam starts filling the lake. Today we went to Montana for such a ceremony—to dedicate a dam.

We flew on *Air Force One* into a very wooded area in the northwest part of the state, then took helicopters from the field where the plane landed to the vicinity of the dam. From the helicopters we transferred to a motorcade that proceeded up to the actual dam site.

As I said before, normally President Nixon kept a fairly reliable schedule, but on this overcast and dreary day we were running almost an hour late for some reason. When our official party arrived at one end of the Libby Dam, we saw there were about a hundred people waiting. Most of them were workmen connected with the project, but one of the important people there was the majority leader of the Senate, Mike Mansfield. It was his dam that was being dedicated.

Once the President had taken a look at the project from the little platform on the edge of the dam, he was ready to start the actual ceremony, which consisted of pouring a bucket of cement into the dam forms. A cement carrier was suspended on a cable from a crane. When it came time to dump the cement, the workmen would pull the rope to

At a dedication ceremony for a Montana dam: President Nixon and Senate Majority Leader Mike Mansfield tugged and tugged, but the bucket of cement wouldn't budge.

open the bottom of the bucket and let the cement pour down into the construction area. The bucket held a substantial amount of concrete—I'd guess a full cubic yard, which is a lot of concrete aggregate.

Everything was ready. President Nixon, Mike Mansfield, and four or five of the workers got hold of a big rope and, looking like they were playing tug of war, started to pull on the rope to open the bottom of the concrete bucket. They held the rope steady so we could photograph the scene for a minute or so. When we were all through, we signaled them to go ahead, and they pulled on the rope. The bottom of the bucket wouldn't move.

As I said, the dedication ceremony had been delayed about an hour. In an hour, remember, a bucket of cement can get pretty hard, and it had done just that. The result was that no matter how much the rope gang pulled and tugged, the bottom of the bucket wouldn't open up and empty its contents down into the dam.

There was a lot of tugging and pulling, but no cigar. Then the whole bunch of dignitaries burst out laughing. Despite more efforts, the concrete still wouldn't budge. Finally, a group of husky workmen took over. They had to climb into the bucket and bang it very hard with shovels until they managed to loosen it up enough so that a big cube of it clunked down into the construction site. A big cheer went up.

One of my jobs as official photographer of the President was to lead the press pool when the President traveled anywhere for a particularly newsworthy event. On big trips, when representatives of many different newspapers and wire services were invited to accompany the President, there was no need for a pool. But for shorter trips, it was the custom to reduce the number of press members to a select few. When you figure that there are about 130 reporters and photographers usually assigned to cover the President of the United States, it isn't surprising that when he goes somewhere he takes along only a limited number of them.

"The real work is done here," said Nixon of his hideaway office in the Executive Office Building. Here he's shown with Henry Kissinger and Mimi, Nixon's poodle.

President Nixon and Henry Kissinger in a doorway conference in the Oval Office. Outside is the Rose Garden.

Secretary of State William P. Rogers and the President in a Rose Garden meeting.

A press "pool" consisted of an AP writer, an AP photographer, a UPI writer, a UPI photographer, a representative of the networks, and a representative of a newspaper. These jobs were rotated so that there were different people in the pool on each assignment.

It was my job to look after the pool: to get them in the bus on time, get them away from the conference hall or whatever on time, and so on. When *Air Force One* landed, the Secret Service ran out first. I ran out next, and the pool followed me. Then we turned around and photographed the rest of the party. After we'd covered the story, when we'd see the President get back in his chopper, we all ran like a bunch of wild banshees to get aboard the flight on time.

The big problem I had was that the local cops would sometimes grab pool members. They would see them running like maniacs, and so naturally a red flag of alarm went up and they grabbed them. Then I would have to go over and tell them to let them go and that I was a member of the President's staff. By throwing my weight around sometimes I got them released, and sometimes I didn't. Hell, I couldn't even get Ron Ziegler released once in Paris. Those gendarmes are a rough, tough bunch.

Being assigned to the President was a far cry from being assigned to the candidate when he was running in 1968. I don't think any candidate took better care of the press than Nixon.

But then something happened.

I was there when the change came about. It had been the custom all during the Presidential campaign for the local Republican committees to serve Danish pastries and coffee in a corner of the press room. The reporters coming down could eat their breakfast while waiting around for the action.

Right after the election, one of the wire service reporters walked into the press room at the hotel in Key Biscayne. He looked over at the snack bar and snorted a couple of times in contempt at the pastries-and-coffee scene. The food was well-picked over by this time, because most of us

President Nixon addressing a sea of young faces at Nebraska State University.

This picture was taken at the White House just before Ed Cox and Tricia Nixon were married.

President Nixon gives a hurried geography lesson to a group of third graders at an elementary school in San Clemente.

Mrs. Nixon was always quick to catch the spirit of local ceremonies. Here she is in a headdress that was presented to her by a group of women in Ghana, West Africa.

had been down there early and had had a couple of cups of coffee and two or three Danishes.

This gentleman waited until Ron Ziegler walked into the room. Then, in a loud, commanding voice, he said, "Mr. Ziegler, if you think you're going to *buy* us by putting out this food, you got another think coming!"

Ziegler was startled, but he didn't say anything.

"We're well able to buy our own food," the reporter continued officiously, "and we're not going to be *bought off* by this breakfast assortment in the mornings. I want you to know that right now."

Ziegler looked him straight in the eye.

"Very well," he said, and that was all he said.

Never again was there coffee and Danish pastry waiting for the members of the press. The food hadn't been put out there to *buy* the press. It had just been another little service the Nixon staff performed, like picking up the bags and putting them on the trucks, and giving out advance schedules. However, if there was a feeling that the Nixon staff was bribing the press, Ziegler was determined to put a stop to it. And he did.

February 20, 1972 / En route to China

On the flight across the Pacific on *Air Force One* which had recently been renamed *The Spirit of '76,* a bunch of us in the pool handed the President a large atlas of China which had been made up for him. Imprinted on the cover was the rather elaborate insignia of the Central Intelligence Agency.

"Do you think they'll let us in China with this CIA thing?" one of the reporters joked.

"Why not?" Nixon responded deadpan. "It may prove to the Chinese how much our people *don't* know about their country."

The few preceding days were so eventful that I didn't have a chance to make many notes about them. We spent the time in Honolulu pretty much like all tourists do. It has always been a paradise for servicemen of all nations, a place to relax and enjoy yourself—and run the risk of getting robbed and beaten if you've got that in mind.

The President went in swimming at the famous beach at Waikiki. After we were back on the plane again, one of the pool reporters asked the President how he had liked the Islands.

"Fine," he said. "The waves were so big I almost got rolled."

I still don't know if it was a joke or just a "Nixonism."

A peek into the Presidential compartment aboard Air Force One *shows President Nixon studying his papers en route to Peking.*

President Nixon, with Mrs. Nixon, being greeted by Premier Chou En-lai at the bottom of the ramp of Air Force One. This moment signaled the end of the long cold war between the United States and China.

February 24, 1972   /   Hangchow, China

In the park at West Lake in Hangchow, the Premier walked this morning with the First Lady just ahead of us, showing her the sights. By the lake we came to a cage containing a pair of lovebirds. The two birds began embracing, rubbing their beaks together, and cooing.

This wasn't in the scenario. Decorum had been violated. The Premier looked stern and flustered.

Pat Nixon smiled and trilled at the birds: "Lovey-dovey!"

Waiting until the President's wife had walked on, the Premier leaned toward the cage and said something in Chinese to the birds.

Mrs. Nixon turned back. "I talk to my birds the same way you do," she told the Premier.

He smiled enigmatically. We never did find out what he had said. It didn't really sound like "lovey-dovey" to me—even in Chinese.

February 25, 1972 / *The Great Wall of China*

As already mentioned, President Nixon never did anything, went any-where, or talked to anyone without being carefully briefed. Even if he was just meeting with the Strawberry Queen, information about who she was, who was sponsoring her, what she represented, her age, school-ing and background, and the purpose of the meeting would be set forth in a backgrounder, which the President painstakingly studied before the meeting took place.

Probably the most complicated of all these briefing arrangements was the one prepared for the President's trip to China. The papers in con-nection with it filled two or three suitcases. The President himself went over all the documents until he knew the historical background back-ward and forward, and the political situation, as analyzed by his State Department experts, inside out.

Everything was covered—all the people he would meet, their names, the phonetic pronunciation of their names, their backgrounds, their job designations and their responsibilities—so he would know exactly what he was doing. He was very intense and serious about every bit of this study.

In the Executive Office Building he looked over this material for many, many hours by himself. When a question came up, he would

The President and Mrs. Nixon, with a large group of U.S. and Chinese officials, strolling atop the Great Wall.

summon one of the people responsible for the specific phase of the study and interrogate him.

As far as I know, he never missed a pronunciation, fluffed a name, or said the wrong thing on the entire trip. He was letter-perfect. Too letter-perfect, maybe. Spontaneity is a difficult thing to come by if you work at it too hard.

Today, when he stood on the Great Wall of China, as the photographers shot pictures and the Chinese officials waited for his reaction, the President mentally searched the reams of information he had waded through about the number of men who gave their lives to build the wall, the millions of tons of rock in it, the length and breadth of it, its age, and so much more, before he finally came up with his eagerly awaited pronouncement:

"This," he said expansively, summing it all up, "is a great wall."

February 26, 1972   /   China

The President was up until 5:00 A.M. this morning working out a communiqué about his talks with Chairman Mao and Chou En-lai. But when I saw him, he appeared surprisingly alert and rested, almost in a festive mood.

I asked him how he managed to keep looking so fit when working so hard.

He smiled faintly. "Some people wear out inside, Ollie, and some wear out outside. I happen to wear out inside."

President Nixon was entertained at a sumptuous banquet in the Great Hall of the People in Peking. Premier Chou En-lai is on his left.

President Nixon posing with the entire press corps that accompanied him to China.

May 22, 1972   /   Moscow, U.S.S.R.

Sitting in my room on the nineteenth floor of the Intourist Hotel in Moscow, I could see the Kremlin from my window. It looks formidable, with the very high fortress-type wall around it, and several identical entrances. Getting into the Kremlin was a real problem for all of us.

I found that it was much smarter not to carry a camera case, because if I did, I was immediately identified as press. However, if I carried a couple of cameras over my shoulder, without any case, I could go pretty much any place I wanted.

It was almost June during our stay and dawn broke about 4:00 A.M. By 4:30 the sun shone brightly over the Kremlin. It didn't get dark until 9:00 P.M., making for a very long day.

Drivers in Moscow are unbelievable. Automobiles have the right of way, and they take it. A man on foot doesn't have a chance.

Even the motorcade coming in from the airport traveled at a cruise speed of 75 miles an hour for the most part. Our driver wasn't what you'd call an expert. The car had push-button transmission similar to what American vehicles had had some years ago. When we started, the driver pushed the reverse button, and, sure enough, the car began backing up. He pushed some more buttons and finally hit the one that moved us forward.

As for the food, the staples are tea and coffee, red cheese, and cold cuts.

President Nixon, Mrs. Nixon, and Secretary of State Rogers attending the Bolshoi ballet in Moscow with the three top Soviet leaders.

Every breakfast is like a picnic. The coffee is a cross between Nescafé and Turkish coffee, with about a half inch of rather strong-tasting sludge that remains at the bottom of the cup.

I opted for tea. Tea leaves float in it, and lemon flavors it. The tea is served in a hot glass and is almost impossible to drink from until it has cooled down rather substantially.

Russian photographers are big burly guys who perform like Redskin tackles when you work with them. I saw one who really hit the police line with all the savvy of a linebacker. Throwing half a dozen other photographers, both American and Russian, to the ground, he plowed through the front line until he was right in front of Pat Nixon; then he began making his shots as casually as you please.

Tonight I saw the Bolshoi doing the best ballet in the world. And probably the longest. But the dancing was great. Even the line girls would be considered prima ballerinas in the States.

The President and the Soviet leaders watched from a box that had had Soviet and American flags appliquéd as decorations on either side. I think the picture I took of the Presidential party was one of the best I'd shot on the trip so far.

President Nixon, the first American president to visit the Soviet Union, broadcasts to the people of the U.S.S.R. from an ornate room in the Kremlin.

May 26, 1972   /   The Kremlin, Moscow

A crisis occurred this morning which could only happen in Russia. I was having breakfast in the Blair House section of the Kremlin when Manolo Sanchez, the President's valet, came barreling in. Wringing his hands, he started babbling half in Spanish and half in English about the Russian cooks. I calmed him down and finally discovered that he was upset because no one knew how to cook an egg.

Mrs. Nixon had ordered a hard-boiled egg. Well, the Russian chefs had cooked nine eggs, but not one of them got to be hard-boiled. Every time Manolo cracked a new one open, he found it was raw and he had to throw it away. He'd tell them then to cook it nine minutes, but to no avail.

At the end of the nine soft-boiled eggs he threw in the sponge. Mrs. Nixon never got her egg.

I had my first experience with Russian satellite eggs in Romania. I was having breakfast at a little hotel where I was staying, and everyone was eating eggs, so I ordered one too. When mine came, it appeared slightly warmed, but no more than you'd expect from the body heat of the chicken itself. I told the guys around the table about it, but they just laughed.

"They don't cook eggs any longer than that," one veteran said. "When

President Nixon and Henry Kissinger walking on the Kremlin grounds after a light rain.

Weary from a long day of negotiations, President Nixon returns to his quarters at the Kremlin.

you're eating eggs in Communist countries, you eat them raw, or you don't eat them at all."

Mrs. Nixon got good press play in Russia. Not only the American but also the Russian press followed her everywhere. She was asked at one point what she thought of the women's styles today as compared to 1959, when she and her husband had been in Russia before.

"They're much the same," she said, nodding approval. Then, realizing that she had inadvertently told the truth—that they were as drab as ever—she immediately said: "I mean, of course, that they are in fashion as always!"

May 28, 1972   /   Moscow, U.S.S.R.

The day started off with church services at a little (would you believe it?) Baptist church in Moscow. The church crowd was made up of about 50 percent parishioners and 50 percent Soviet agents. The area was roped off for several blocks, so that no one but the invited parties could get in. The only ones who had trouble were members of the press, few of whom were let inside.

By 7:00 A.M. the church was full. Then Russian agents cleared out one balcony on the pretext that it was reserved for the press. But of course, there wasn't any press there.

Since no cameras were permitted, I had tucked mine under my raincoat. Ron Ziegler told me to sweep in just behind the President. Then an official from the U.S. embassy was going to direct me down to the front of the church, where I could sneak a few shots during the service.

My escort, whom I had never seen before, was Robin Porter of the U.S. embassy. Bill Henkel of the advance contingent pointed him out to me. Porter got me a chair and seated me up front with a lot of little old Russian ladies. The President and Mrs. Nixon sat some fifteen feet away from me. During the hymn singing I reached down and sneaked out my cameras from under my raincoat. I tried to be discreet as I made the shots.

Frankly, I thought that I was going to be grabbed by the KGB at any moment. But I wasn't. The service, which went on for two hours, was preached all in Russian and of course meant little to most of the American party. During the last hymn Porter came down and directed me up to the rear of the church, where I took a couple of shots of the interior.

When the Nixons got up to leave, four very burly Soviet guards formed a line six or seven feet wide in front of them to lead them out, so it was impossible for me to get a good clean shot of them departing. All in all, it was a bit hairy working with cameras inside the church. Those Soviet agents are a rude and rough-and-ready bunch. And since quite a few of them are women, you never really know who's an agent and who a smiling housewife.

Tonight we experienced a typical example of Soviet harassment. The President was scheduled to make a television broadcast to the Russian people from the Green Room of the Kremlin. The national director of Soviet television was in charge and had told us that he would let only one U.S. 16mm. television film camera document the speech on sound film.

When the crew showed up at the Kremlin, it was admitted to the Rose Room, the chamber adjacent to the Green Room. At that point, everything looked, you might say, rosy.

But the Rose Room was as far as they ever got. As the time for the President's address got closer, the crew began arguing with the guards. The loud hassling reached a crescendo at the moment Nixon began to speak, and then it ended, of course. There was no point fighting after that.

A Soviet photographer with a still camera clicked off about half a dozen shots during the broadcast. That was the total coverage.

The President, no doubt unaware of what had gone on between the Russians and us in the other room, seemed as cool as a cucumber on television.

Even after the broadcast it wasn't easy to get any picture-taking organized. Ron Ziegler had instructed Bob Taylor of the Secret Service to get the photographic pool up to the Green Room right after the speech, but the pool was held up at some remote checkpoint in the Kremlin. When it looked as if there would be no afterspeech coverage at all, suddenly a big set of immense double doors opened and all members of the photographic pool were finally herded in like cattle.

I was lead man. However, one of the Soviet guards standing in front of the door decided to snatch me. It was no good trying to plow on by him—he was as strong as an ox. Also, I was carrying a lot of expensive equipment and I certainly didn't want to have a fist fight right in front of the President.

Dwight Chapin, just ahead of me, saw what was happening and came over and grabbed the guard's arm. At that point a couple of agents came up behind me to take me away. Chapin pushed the first guard up against the wall like a torpedo in one of those old Jimmy Cagney movies. With the agents in back of me pressing in and the first guard out of the way, I slipped on through.

And I got my shots. Always the hard way.

May 29, 1972 / Kiev, U.S.S.R.

We got to Kiev, our last stop in Russia, late because the Russian aircraft leaving Moscow developed an engine problem. All was confusion because the President's motorcade went directly to his residence, and the press pool went directly to the press hotel. I was in the last bus, and realized I'd never get over in time to organize press pool coverage of the banquet. So I radioed ahead and instructed Bob Knudsen, who had taken the first bus, to get the press pool over to the banquet. I learned later what happened at the banquet.

As soon as the dinner started, the entire pool of photographers was driven out. I mean, literally. They were told, in no uncertain terms, to leave. Knudsen, whose instructions are to play it very cool in such explosive situations, decided to go without making an issue of it.

Meanwhile, knowing nothing of all this, I was getting myself settled in my hotel, which was jumping with foreign, American, and Russian press. Every room in the place was packed. Five minutes after the last bus arrived, most of us decided to forget the banquet.

I got squared away, washed up, and went downstairs to eat dinner. When I got back to my room, it was about ten. I sank onto the bed and thought: *Man, this is great. I'm going to get a good night's sleep for a change.*

I was standing there in my drawers stretching and yawning when all of a sudden my beeper came alive.

I telephoned signal and identified myself.

"Searchlight wants Hawkeye to report to the banquet immediately," said signal. Searchlight was the President's code name for the trip. "He wants pictures immediately."

"Hawkeye is at the press hotel at least a half hour away. Impossible to comply." I told him to locate Knudsen with the press pool and assign him the job. I had no inkling, of course, that Knudsen and the rest of the photographers were now back in the same hotel I was in.

A full five minutes passed before I was beeped again. "Hawkeye," said the operator, "we can't locate anyone."

I threw up my hands.

But we got the pictures, anyway.

How?

Brigadier General Walter Tkach, the President's personal physician, likes to use one of my cameras with a built-in meter during overseas trips. It's a little tourist-model $12.50 job called an Instamatic.

He told me later what finally happened at the banquet.

"The President suddenly got the idea of doing his favorite thing: 'Setting Up a Picture.' You know how he likes to do that. Just before things began to break up, he got the entertainers, the Russian diplomats, and the American staff members all together for a big group shot.

"I looked around for you and discovered to my horror that you weren't at the banquet. Haldeman then told me that the entire photography pool had been kicked out. I could see what would happen when the President got everybody grouped together, glanced up to look for a sea of cameras and flash bulbs, and find nothing.

"I rushed out into the limousine, grabbed up my mini-flash, and ran back in just in time to see the President turn around and signal for the camera crew that wasn't there to begin.

"There was a moment's hushed silence when he looked straight into my eyes and saw the little insignificant snapshot camera in my hands. He turned just a little pale. Then he shook himself, played it cool, like a veteran actor whose prop gun won't fire, and smiled while I knocked off a half-dozen flash shots.

"I played Ollie Atkins, and when it was all over, I called across the banquet hall: 'Thank you, Mr. President,' and walked out."

And that's how I covered the banquet in Kiev.

John Ehrlichman and Ron Ziegler conferring on Air Force One.

Henry Kissinger presides at a secret meeting of the National Security Council in the basement of the White House.

May 30, 1972 / Iran

I missed the best picture of my life when I didn't manage to get a shot of the belly dancer jumping onto Henry Kissinger's lap at a late-night party in a joint in Teheran.

Kissinger never lets an opportunity for a press quote go by. When asked what he thought of "Nadia"—a name as common as Mary is in America—the chief of the National Security Council said: "A charming girl. We discussed the conversion tables of the strategic arms limitations agreement."

May 31, 1972 / Warsaw, Poland

We arrived in downtown Warsaw in the morning. We didn't bother about taking any pictures, but when the Presidential limousine stopped at a kind of housing project, we got out and made a few crowd shots. It wasn't worth it. The Polish gestapo is a rough bunch, ruder even than the Moscow variety.

Finally we went into Old Warsaw and wound up at an enormous public square, where thousands of people had gathered. Very close to the tomb of the Unknown Soldier, a simple ceremony was performed. The President hung a wreath, in what has become a standard GI performance in Europe since World War II. It's boring for the photographers and reporters, but they cover it anyway.

Meanwhile, the Polish crowd was really being held at bay by a police line. It's unusual in these countries to see people defying the police, so we were amazed when those lines started getting bulges in them. I took a couple pictures of the struggle. Then I jumped in a car that looked like a nineteen-twenties gangster's convertible, and we drove about a block before the President stopped again.

It was really amazing. He got out of the car and began moving through the people—"pressing the flesh," as we say. He shook hands with the people and waved at them, and some of them broke through the gestapo line.

We all got some shots of the bone-bruising rugby match that we went to next. The main idea was to take some pictures, but not get hurt.

Bob Haldeman came out of the mess with a gashed forehead. Dwight Chapin had a black eye. Herb Klein had a couple of bad bruises, but I walked away with no big problem except a pretty bad tear in my coat. I actually had ripped it when I was jumping off the pool limousine.

The press had occasion today to play golf with the President, and it was a sight to see. The game took place after an early-day visit of Teamsters Union officials at the Western White House.

Everybody was packing up, when the President, on impulse, decided to play a few holes on his own practice course. He invited the press pool along, and so we all trooped off with him.

The course is a very small five-hole layout, with one tee located right off the end of the swimming pool. That's actually the first tee, the green for which is about 175 yards away.

The President figured that a 7 iron would be about the right club for him to use for this drive. He invited us all to go up with him and watch.

Then he got a better idea. "I'll give a special prize to anyone who gets a hole in one," he said. "I'll give a beautiful set of golf clubs with the President's name inscribed on them to the winner."

We took this all in stride as the President went up to the tee with a 7 iron and ball. "Here," he said. "I'll show you how it's done."

He teed up the ball and slammed one that went only about halfway up to the green.

A couple of the press people laughed.

"Obviously," said the President, "that's not the way to be a real golf

A portrait of President Nixon in the atrium at San Clemente.

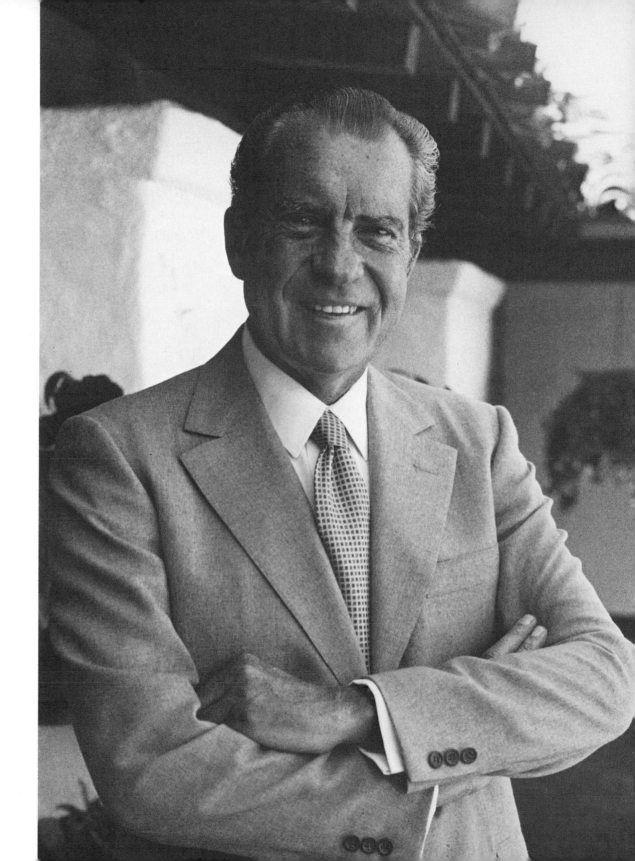

pro. Every man is entitled to a practice shot." He laughed. "I'll now take my regular shot."

He put the second ball up, addressed himself to it, and hooked it to the left. He was so far off that he didn't get anywhere near the green.

"All right," he said. "We'll make it three."

He gave the third ball a good solid whack, and it went high enough, but it didn't go far enough to reach the green.

"I had a crack at it," he said, "and now I'm going to let all of you try it."

At first nobody would take him up on the offer, but finally a couple of brave souls lined up. I don't know who was first, but whoever it was sliced it way over into the garden area. He gave up and a second expert didn't get up to the green either.

Whether it was the place, the audience, the martinis we had all consumed beforehand, or something else, I can't say, but everybody was off his game. Even the best player in the press pool, a writer for the Scripps-Howard Newspapers who really is a doggone good golfer, slugged away at a couple of miserable shots. First he overdrove the green, then he landed in a trap, and finally he chopped the ball and it rolled slowly along the lawn in front of him. Everybody laughed.

Nixon shook his head. "I tell you what I'm going to do," he said. "I'm going to throw in the golf carts too, if anyone gets a hole in one."

So a couple more of them tried, but nobody made it in two, much less one.

One newsman's wife turned to her husband and said, "If he throws in La Casa Pacifica, that might give us some incentive."

Whatever the stakes, nobody was able to get close. In fact, for my money, it was the most miserable exhibition of golfing I've ever seen.

August 22, 1972   /   Miami, Florida

It's convention time again. The President was remaining secluded at Key Biscayne until called on to make his acceptance address.

Tonight Sammy Davis Jr. and a large group of other entertainers were conducting a youth rally at the Miami Marina, a stadium built out in the water for aquatic shows like powerboat races and swim events. At the close of the jazz rally run by Sammy Davis Jr., President Nixon made an unexpected appearance. It was a surprise to the entertainers and to the kids, but the rest of us had known he was going to do it.

I was right there with him when he walked up on the stage and Sammy Davis Jr. welcomed him with open arms. I got a shot of that. Later on, the entertainer grabbed the President in a big bear hug from the back, and I made a really spectacular picture of that.

There were other shots showing the President at the microphone with Sammy Davis Jr. standing to the rear and behind him just a little bit, with all the kids perched around on the background scenery. Those were rather unusual pictures to make of the President, because most of the youngsters were wearing the scantiest of clothing. There was nothing indecent about it, though; it was just the typical dress for entertainment personalities.

Sammy Davis Jr. had a little Kodak Instamatic. He announced to the audience that he was a photographer for *Jet* magazine and took a picture of the President. When he was through, the President grabbed the camera from him and made a photograph of him. "Maybe you can put me on the staff!" he laughed.

(99)

August 27, 1972   /   San Clemente, California

A celebrities reception was held at the Western White House tonight in honor of the President's renomination at the Republican Convention in Miami. Over four hundred prominent Hollywood personalities were invited to meet the President and Mrs. Nixon.

The receiving line was a photographer's dream. As the guests were coming up, they were being entertained by a Marimba band, which was very good, very Mexican, and very Southern Californian. The line then went into the courtyard of La Casa Pacifica where the President and First Lady greeted each guest individually.

Taft Schreiber, director of MCA (Music Corporation of America), the giant talent agency, introduced the guests to the President and the President chatted with each one for a few moments. After moving on to shake hands with Mrs. Nixon, the guests walked over to the swimming pool area, where the reception was being held.

I photographed each guest with the President—over four hundred people. What surprised me was that even these show business people, who are used to being at functions with prominent people, were slightly in awe of meeting the President of the United States. Later, when the photographs had been printed, the President autographed them and had them sent to the guests. It took the President an hour and fifteen minutes to greet all the guests, who included, among so many others, Debbie

Reynolds, Jimmy Durante, and Martin and Rowan of the television "Laugh-In" show.

Another receiving line started at the close of the affair down by the edge of the swimming pool. Guests came up to thank the President before leaving. When I saw Zsa Zsa Gabor and Eva Gabor both talking to the President at the same time, I realized it was too good an opportunity to miss. I made a shot of them.

Zsa Zsa, who misses nothing, came over later on.

"You took pictures," she said. "Are you sure you've got film in your camera?"

"I'm sure."

"I want to have a copy of that picture."

I told her I could promise that.

"By the way," she added, "Bebe Rebozo said he would pose with me."

We found Bebe in a few minutes and I took a picture of Zsa Zsa with him.

I noticed Bob Taylor, head of the Secret Service detail in charge of the President's personal guard, standing about a foot away from the President, ready to grab him if he happened to back off into the pool.

It didn't happen. Nor did any guests fall in. I saw a few who were very close to the edge and warned them to look out.

Another Presidential tradition—this one initiated under Kennedy—flouted.

Writing about the San Clemente reception reminds me of another reception. I had taken pictures the same as I did tonight, and when I got back to Washington, a very prominent Hollywood entertainer approached me in my office at the White House.

"You took pictures of me at San Clemente," he said.

I said I had and asked him if he wanted a copy.

"Not exactly," he said. "In fact, I would like the negative."

I can't remember his exact words, but he explained that the woman he had been photographed with wasn't really his wife. She was either someone else's wife, or someone whom he had taken there. In any case, he didn't want the fact recorded for posterity.

I promised him nothing, but discussed the matter with Ron Ziegler, who tossed it around with somebody on the President's staff. The upshot of it was that I had the lab clip out one frame from my roll and reprint the set of contacts with the number and I.D. on the next frame.

So much for top-secret documents and cover-ups in the White House.

September 9, 1972   /   Wilkes-Barre, Pennsylvania

Leaving the house about eight, we drove up to Camp David, arriving at nine-thirty. A meeting had been scheduled for ten between the President and Frank Carlucci, the White House aide responsible for helping clean up the disastrous Wilkes-Barre flood in Pennsylvania.

When we got to the New Conference Hall, we found that the President was still asleep. Ten minutes to ten, and he still hadn't shown up. "Who's going to wake the President?" the staff members kept asking each other, tossing it back and forth at each other like a hot potato.

A Coast Guard aide finally woke him and got him to the meeting with Carlucci. John Ehrlichman came out, got me, and I went in and made three frames of the two of them, jumped in my car, and drove to Washington, where I took the films to the lab for processing.

Returning to the press office to see what my instructions were, if any, I found Bebe Rebozo there. He invited me in to the Executive Mess for a cup of coffee, and we killed about fifteen minutes talking. Suddenly Ehrlichman appeared in the doorway.

"Ollie," he said, coming over to us, "I'm glad you're here. Get on *Chopper Number One*. We're going up to Wilkes-Barre, Pennsylvania. Take plenty of film."

I grabbed my gear and climbed onto *Number One* with the President, Ehrlichman, Frank Carlucci, and a couple of reporters.

At Wilkes-Barre we landed in a schoolyard and motorcaded to a small college nearby, where the President was going to present three million dollars in repair money to counteract the damage that the hurricane Agnes flood had caused.

I took pictures and looked around. A little black girl came up to the President. She told him that her organization was going to have a picnic the following Sunday, at which hot dogs and root beer would be served.

"Are you going to have enough hot dogs?" the President asked her, making conversation off the top of his head.

"I'm not sure that we will have," she said.

The President hesitated, but turned to John Ehrlichman. "John," he said, "I want you to be sure that these people have enough hot dogs and supplies for their picnic next week."

"Yes sir," said Ehrlichman, making notes on his yellow lined pad.

"I'll pay for it," the President went on.

On a tour of the damaged area through Wilkes-Barre side streets, we came to the old section of the city. The flood waters had got into the walls of the old frame houses and had so bulged out the plaster and lath that most of the structures would have to be entirely rebuilt.

People were already at work in some of the homes. The President stopped at one house where the owner and his wife were busy repairing the walls. The woman had a trowel in her hand.

Her husband told us he was a railroad worker.

Inside we could see that all the plasterboard was torn off the studs; there was nothing left but the 2 x 4's. It is really easier to build a whole new house than repair one afflicted by major flood damage of that kind.

I made pictures while the reporters talked to the man and his wife. I took one of the President inside the house, one of him outside next to the wall, and another of him standing by a huge hole in the street that had been made by the raging flood waters.

A group of Army Corps of Engineers personnel was working bull-dozers and dump trucks, helping clear up the mess. The President chatted with them for a while, and I took pictures.

We continued cruising around the city by automobile, visiting additional flooded areas that were now dry but littered with debris. While on the main street we passed a United Presbyterian church. It was about one in the afternoon and a wedding was in progress. The married couple's bridesmaids and friends were lined up on the front steps.

When the President stopped the motorcade and got out, I knew immediately he was heading over to talk to the bride and groom. I jumped out of the press car and ran over to the church ahead of him, taking a picture as he strode over toward the entrance.

I told a woman who was standing just inside the church doorway looking out, "The President of the United States is about to walk up here."

She looked aghast, but then she recognized Nixon and began to get excited.

"Let's get the bride and groom out here on the step," I said. "I'm going to take pictures. It will be quite an event."

"I'll get them," the woman said.

The young couple soon appeared. She had apparently briefed them because they just stood there and waited.

"Stay on the top step," I instructed them. "The President will come up to you."

After Nixon had climbed the church steps, I took pictures, and while I was at it someone began throwing rice over the bride and groom. I even got rice in my eye, and in one of my pictures the bride and groom are squinting because of the rice.

"Oh boy!" said the groom. "When I put on a wedding, I put it on right. Even the President of the United States comes."

The President chatted with the bride and groom a few minutes, and then we all got back in the motorcade and headed for the helicopter at the airport. It had flown there from the schoolyard, where we originally landed.

I reached home about eight-thirty after a 13½-hour day.

Typical.

September 10, 1972   /   Mirbellville, Maryland

On this very hot Sunday we went on a secret picnic with the Italian American Spaghetti Association out in Maryland. The President flew by helicopter from Camp David, but I was picked up at my home by a White House car and driven around the Beltway. After some difficulty the driver found the place: the Casa Roma, an old folks home and clinic run by the Catholic Church.

At the site where the President's helicopter landed, the President and Secretary of Transportation John A. Volpe were met by a priest. They made their way to the festival site through such a determined crowd that it was hard following the President. Finally we got through to a small stage, where the President made a few brief remarks. There were more than 10,000 guests there.

While he was speaking, I went over to one of the half-dozen festival booths nearby and found that they were putting Italian sausages in hot-dog rolls. I got inside the booth to tell the fellow in charge that I expected the President to come over for a sausage. When he did, I said, I would try to shoot a picture as the roll was being given him.

By the time the President came over to the booth the crowd had packed in so tightly that he could only get within ten or twelve feet of it. The proprietor put a sausage on a paper plate and sent it to the President through the crowd, hand over hand, the way it's done at a football game. On its way to him, a sea of hands was reaching up to get a hold of the sausage. All he could see was the bottom of the paper plate. And he never did get the sausage.

I stuck my camera on the end of a pole and pushed it out over the crowd. I tracked the sausage on its trip to the President, with his face down below, and thought I had a good picture. It didn't turn out as dramatically as I would have liked it to, but it wasn't too bad. Anyway, it was the most dramatic thing about the spaghetti festival.

The President had a visitor by the name of Marian Skully today—a little Irish girl, probably fourteen or fifteen years old. She's the daughter of the farmer who owned the field where the President's helicopter landed on a recent trip to Ireland. (That was the trip when we went over to visit the old Nixon cemetery.) The girl is visiting the United States for six weeks. Ron Ziegler figured we could get a good picture of her with one of the President's dogs.

After they had brought Timahoe, the Irish setter, up from the kennels, the President, the little Irish lass, and the dog went out on the porch outside the President's office to make a picture. The press pool was corralled in the hallway outside the President's office waiting with Jack Darcy of the press office.

As soon as we were set up, I gave Jack the motion to send the photographers out. By this time the President had Timahoe by his leash and the little Irish girl was standing by him. She was petting the dog, and he seemed to be behaving himself.

The photographers made a few shots of the President with the little girl and the dog while the girl patted the dog on the head. Then the President, on impulse, decided to show off his dog. "Tim, sit!" he ordered him.

Tim paid absolutely no attention in the manner of dogs from time eternal. The President commanded again: "Tim, sit!" He said it a little louder and more firmly the second time. The dog paid no attention whatsoever. "Sit, Tim!" he said for the third time. Nothing.

After the sixth time, Ziegler thought he'd give it a try. "Tim, sit!" he said. The dog turned around to see who else was bothering him with a new voice, but that was all. He didn't sit.

Manolo Sanchez, standing in the doorway to the President's office watching, joined in. "Tim, sit! Tim, sit! Tim, sit!" Even with that voice commanding him, Tim didn't sit. He began panting, though. Well, it was rather warm.

The President got a bright idea. "Manolo," he said, "he doesn't understand English. Tell him in Spanish to sit. Then he'll sit."

Manolo told him in Spanish to sit. The dog did nothing. Whereupon Manolo went up to Tim, grabbed him firmly by the nose, and put a gentle hand on his butt. Raising his nose and pushing his butt, he made him sit. Tim sat, and he stayed seated.

The photographers of course were shooting this episode with a great deal of enjoyment.

Ziegler had turned pale. He was worried that on film it would appear that Manolo Sanchez was slapping the dog, somehow manhandling Tim.

Yet that is really the way dogs are trained. You push their butts down and lift their heads to make them sit. Normally you use the lead, but the President had the lead, so Manolo had to grab Tim by the nose.

When this session was over, I had just got down to the office when I had an emergency call from Ziegler. I trotted up to see him immediately.

"Ollie," he said, "did it look like Manolo was slapping or beating the President's dog?"

"It didn't look that way to me," I said. "That's the way trainers make dogs sit. They put a hand on the butt and push it down and raise the head by the leash a little bit. I see nothing wrong there."

"You remember LBJ and the beagles and the ear-holding flap?" Ziegler asked. "Are we going to go through all that again?"

"I don't think so, Ron," I said.

"Go out there and talk to those photographers and see what they think," he told me.

I went out and approached the only photographer still there. "How did that picture look to you?" I asked him, trying not to tip my mitt.

"All right, nothing special," he said.

"Did you get the picture of the dog straining on the leash?"

"I was changing lenses when that happened, so I missed it."

"Did you get him sitting?"

"Yes. I made one shot of him sitting. It's not much of a picture."

I went back and told Ron Ziegler that the picture was no big crush in the mind of the photographers. "I wouldn't worry about it."

"All right," he said. "Rush your film down to the lab and print everything on it. I want to see the roll."

I went down to the office and sent the film over to the lab.

Then I got another call up to Ziegler's office.

"He's so very much worried about it, you know," Ziegler told me, referring to Nixon. "He really feels he's blown it this time."

I said, "Ron, you'll have the film down here as soon as it's processed. As far as I can see, I don't think you have cause for concern."

And that was that.

When the pictures finally came, I took them up to him. Sure enough, there was one with Manolo holding the dog by the snout, pushing his butt down. It didn't look unkind to the dog at all. Anyhow, that night I checked both TV networks, but neither used the film of the dog. I thought there might be something in the paper the next day, because the press runs a lot more pictures than the networks do. But I was sure it wasn't going to cause the commotion that the LBJ beagle incident caused.

And I was right. No flap ensued. In fact, nobody even said anything.

November 11-22, 1972 / Camp David, Maryland

The President went to Camp David following his return from Key Biscayne, where he had gone shortly after the election. I then found myself commuting from McLean, my home, to this mountain area.

Camp David was Franklin Delano Roosevelt's old "Shangri-La" hideaway, where he worked during World War II, away from the pressures of Washington. It was President Eisenhower who renamed the place Camp David.

It had been an old boot camp for navy recruits back in the 1930s. And in spite of the fact that it's quite comfortable in the winter, it was built like a summer place, with rustic structures and simple furnishings.

The President really had two cottages at Camp David. They were called "lodges," in the frontier tradition. He preferred the one called Aspen Lodge although a rather pretentious new one, about four months old, had been put together for him: New Laurel.

He was spending time here reorganizing the government and changing the Cabinet and White House staff in preparation for his second term. I was up to shoot important members of the Cabinet and other office holders visiting the President.

I missed Secretary of State Bill Rogers, who paid a surprise visit that was such a surprise I didn't even know about it. But I got just about everybody else.

Yet, it wasn't easy.

New Laurel had been built with a spacious office for the President and a big room that might be used for Cabinet meetings. There was also a large living room with a free-standing fireplace, an executive dining room, and places for the staff to hang out.

In spite of all this, the President preferred to stay at Aspen Lodge. Not only is Aspen Lodge much smaller, but, unfortunately, there is no facility there for the White House staff, no room for the normal White House operation, and no place for me to hang out except in the kitchen.

It isn't even a lodge, strictly speaking. It's a luxurious home with a heated swimming pool from which mist rises at all times in cold weather such as we were having. The whole operation was run out of the kitchen. In an apparent hangover from the days when the place was strictly a naval camp, this kitchen had two Filipino navy cooks plus a navy enlisted man who wore a red coat and was the waiter. There were also several military aides; John Dettbarn, the commander of Camp David; and me.

For a mess kitchen, it was small—about 10′ x 16′. It was always crowded with people, as well as a butler's pantry right next to it.

A military aide on duty was responsible for the movement of the visitors in and out of the President's office. The aide brought them to Aspen from Laurel, got them in to see the President, and then took them back down to Laurel, whereupon he picked up the next ones.

You can imagine the logistic problems involved. There were two White House phones in the Aspen Lodge kitchen. One hung in the hall in a little coat closet entryway to the kitchen; the other was in the kitchen proper. Both phones were always busy. Someone was on at least one of them at all times, and sometimes they were both in use, occasionally by the same person. More than once I saw one man with a phone at each ear.

When Manolo answered the phone, with his weird sense of humor, he would say: "This is Aspen kitchen, I am Manolo. It's also the photo office, the aide's office, and the kennel."

The President and Vice-President Agnew greeting each other in the doorway to Aspen Lodge at Camp David.

President Nixon reading a paper in front of a picture window at Aspen Lodge.

And he wasn't kidding about the kennel. The Presidential dogs were usually in the kitchen, stretched out asleep on the floor, the three of them: big Timahoe; Vicki, the French poodle; and Pasha, a Yorkshire terrier who looked like a small dustmop.

Whenever I went through the kitchen, I did a tango step, hopping over the dogs and walking around guys who were cooking ducks or basting them, while carrying camera equipment balanced precariously on my shoulder at the same time.

During this stay, for example, the cooks were making a birthday cake for Bebe Rebozo and cooking various things for the President and his guests. I knew nothing about cooking. I could charcoal a steak, but that was about the end of it.

They told me it was a pineapple upside-down cake and that it had already been baked and shaken out of the pan. The parts all looked pretty rough to me, but the chefs said they would trim the sides, cover the cake with frosting, and no one would know the difference. So they said. The chef who was making roses for the top of the cake said he would use four different-colored frostings.

Bebe Rebozo knew the party was for him. He had brought up a briefcase full of things to work on. Camp David was a great retreat for him as well as for the President. Here he could get away from the jungle of the phones, do a lot of thinking, and also take care of all those papers in his briefcase.

Bebe told me that the President wanted me to make some pictures of him in the hydrofoil boat Leonid Brezhnev gave him as a gift. I had already taken pictures of Henry Kissinger on that boat down in the Anacostia River a couple months before.

We had been in front of the Washington Navy Yard. The problem was that the waters were as calm as a millpond. The area there is only two miles in length and a half a mile wide. A hydrofoil is built to go long distances at great speed. By the time they'd get the boat opened up to flat-out speed at Anacostia, it would be time to cut it off.

Soviet Ambassador Anatoly Dobrynin and Henry Kissinger were on the Russian hydrofoil. I was in a jet chase boat manned by the commander of the Anacostia naval installation, trying to take pictures of them. The waves from the hydrofoil were hitting my chase boat, which was trailing slightly behind. The hydrofoil would lift out of the water about six inches or so, but I was being buffeted around so much at that speed that I had to shoot each frame at about 1/2,000 of a second, the highest speed on my Nikons.

I got a few decent pictures. I also got very wet.

Bebe said that Brezhnev had called the President and asked him whether he enjoyed the boat, and if so, would he please send any pictures he had.

"All you have to do, Bebe," I said, "is tell me when you're down there, give me a chase boat, and I'll make the pictures for Comrade Brezhnev."

So, as it stood, I expected to make the pictures on the next trip. But no date had been set yet.

November 23, 1972   /   Camp David, Maryland

By now we've been up here almost twelve days. The President left for New York last weekend for a family get-together. His schedule included going by his law firm in New York, seeing a play, watching a hockey game, and doing a little Christmas shopping.

Today, Thanksgiving, I had a big turkey dinner in the enlisted men's mess along with Major General Walter Tkach, the President's physician, and Commander John Dettbarn.

True to form, the President surprised us by appearing suddenly, saying hello to everybody, and making a few kind remarks. The staff was so astonished by his unexpected appearance that they didn't even get up and clap.

Mrs. Nixon and Julie had also come. While I was shooting a few general scenes showing the President in the enlisted men's mess chatting with the men, Commander Craig Campbell, another aide, beckoned to me. I made my way around the dining hall, and Craig told me that Julie wanted to make some shots of the President with the dogs at Aspen Lodge.

It was four-thirty, overcast, with snow flurries, and the light was absolutely miserable. The sun set between four-thirty and five, so you could imagine the situation photographically, particularly since Julie wanted color pictures. I left black and white in the camera anyway. Walking back to Aspen Lodge from the mess with the President, I shot a few black and whites and took meter readings from the built-in meter as I did so, in anticipation of what I was going to do with color and the dogs.

Then Manolo showed up with the three dogs. Two red ribbons and a green ribbon had been sent out from the White House and were tied on the dogs' collars. The dogs were on leashes for the President to hold.

I could imagine the President struggling with these three vigorous animals, so I suggested to Julie that it might be wise if the three of them —the President, Mrs. Nixon, and Julie—each held one dog and walked along the pathway together. Julie countered that Tricia would be left out of this "almost-family" picture and suggested that only the President and Mrs. Nixon be in the shots with the dogs.

"All right," I said. "Turn the two small dogs over to Mrs. Nixon and give the big dog, Timahoe, to the President to hold."

Manolo was standing behind me. "Wiggle your ears, Manolo," I kidded him, "and make the dogs look at you."

He must have done something, because, sure enough, they looked at him and began walking forward toward him. It made a great shot.

But me? I was scared. I had a great photographic situation, but no light—and I was shooting in color. I shot that color film, rated at 80 ASA, at 400 ASA! That means I had to jump the exposure *four times* its rated capacity.

A very rare press conference—in the helicopter hangar at Camp David.

November 24, 1972   /   Camp David

I worried all night. In the morning when Bob Moore walked in, I said, "Bob, here's a roll of problem color film. I can't tell you what's on it, but there are some very valuable pictures there, if you can bring them out."

I told him the exposure I had used and briefed him on the situation I'd labored under.

Bob knew what to do. "We'll strip off about four or five inches of it and run it through at 400 ASA. Then we'll develop the rest accordingly and see if we can get something."

"Take it down to the lab with you personally and put it in the soup," I told him, "and call me on the phone when you see the sample."

He did. He said they weren't bad. "I think I'll give it just a little more to add a bit of punch. The color balance will be bad, but we'll get a picture."

Getting a picture is what counts in this business. You can make it through the bottom of a Pepsi Cola bottle as long as you get your picture.

At Camp David, Marine Corps aide Jack Brennan directs John Ehrlichman to his quarters, with Bob Haldeman coming up behind.

President Nixon and British Prime Minister Edward Heath take a walk on a foggy day at Camp David.

January 5, 1973 / Washington, D.C.

Memorial services for President Truman were held at the National Cathedral today. President Nixon, who had already gone to the Truman Library, where the body was, and laid a wreath there at the casket, didn't feel any obligation to go to the memorial services.

Foreign dignitaries from many countries were coming to the service, and several of them were scheduled to make courtesy calls upon the President afterward. This put the President in a foul humor. He didn't want to see these people; it really wasn't necessary. He felt that they were taking advantage of him at a time when his mind was preoccupied with a million other things in connection with the Vietnam war.

Ron Ziegler, however, thought each man was important enough to warrant a press photo. So he had announced to the press the day before that there would be a press photo opportunity at the beginning of each meeting. I was told to shoot it all in black and white and color. Bob Knudsen whom I'd brought up with me was to make the color, and I was to do the black and white. We assumed the press would be in on every one of the shots.

However, just before we started, we found out from Steve Bull that the President had canceled the press photo opportunities. Either he had not okayed them to begin with, or if he had okayed them, he had suddenly changed his mind and decided not to. Anyway the press was now in the hallway outside Ziegler's office, ready to go in and take the first picture. I told Jack Darcy, who was in charge of the press, that he had better talk to Steve Bull, because I understood the press was not going in. Jack went in to see Steve, and Steve told him what the President had said. Then Jack ran back and told Ziegler.

Ziegler came back and walked in to see the President. It must have been an interesting conversation because Ziegler came out a subdued man, without a thing to say to anyone. He walked through the hall, disappeared into his office, and that was the end of that.

Darcy had the job of telling the press that the plans were changed; there were to be no pictures after all. A large number of press people had showed because the event had been announced a day in advance.

Amid all this uproar, the last thing in the world I wanted to do was burst into the President's office, make a whole lot of shots, and get him mad at me too. So when the first gentleman came, the Prime Minister of Israel, I went in real quiet, focused the camera, and clicked off one frame, then got out of there fast. As far back as I could remember, that was the only time I had ever made only one frame in the President's office.

The next time I went in I turned my motor on continuous and knocked off two or three frames so that the rest of the dignitaries got two or three shots.

January 6, 1973   /   Washington, D.C.

I slept late. At noon my page boy beeped, meaning that I was to call the signal board immediately. Jerry Warren, the deputy press secretary, was looking for me.

"Ollie," he said, "I hate to do this, but it seems that the pictures we didn't make yesterday for the press have become an international emergency."

"So?"

"I think you better open up the lab and run off a few prints of each one of the people who were in there yesterday afternoon. You can turn them over to me and I'll supply them to the press. That should ease some of the pain down there."

I called my people and went down myself to edit the stuff. A couple of hours later I had everything in Jerry's hands.

January 29, 1973 / Key Biscayne, Florida

Today we went to Florida for a long weekend after two weeks of hectic inaugural business and cease-fire activity, and the LBJ funeral ceremonies. Robert Abplanalp, a personal friend of the President who owns two islands in the Bahamas, had invited the President over.

Abplanalp is a millionaire from the Bronx who made his money from the development of the aerosol spray valve. His two islands are Grand Cay and Walker Cay. Walker Cay is a fishing resort headquarters; the island of Grand Cay is just south of it.

Usually the President splits up the staff and sends the press to Walker Cay, reserving Grand Cay for his immediate family and staff intimates. He stays in a large white house that stands on the high ground of Grand Cay.

This time the President told Manolo Sanchez: "Manolo, go out and catch me some yellowtails and we'll have fresh fish for supper."

Manolo was able to get three rather small yellowtail fish, which he brought back to the Key Biscayne place. At Walker Cay I caught myself a fourteen-pound grouper. The press corps ate that one. When he found out, the President said if he'd known, he'd have asked for my fish to bolster up Manolo's catch. He may have been kidding, but I think he meant it.

(*125*)

I took the chopper from Andrews Air Force Base over to the White House to get my car, which was parked there. Inside the chopper was the President, Mrs. Nixon, and Julie, and the three dogs. Julie had one of the dogs, Pasha, alongside her, and a half-open book lay on the seat. When I first stepped in, it looked to me as if the dog was reading the book. That was good for a laugh.

Just after bringing out one of the President's guests, I spotted Manolo outside the President's office; there was a big lipstick stain on his right cheek.

"Manolo," I said, "what goes here? Are you going in and out of the President's office with that big kiss mark on your cheek?"

"Yes. I'm doing that. And I have a purpose."

"I should think you'd wipe it off. It looks ridiculous."

"There's nothing ridiculous about it at all," he said in his strong Spanish accent. "Today is my birthday. The President is going to see that kiss mark on my cheek and he's going to say just what you did: 'Do you know there's a big kiss mark of lipstick on your cheek?' I'm going to say, 'Yes sir, Mr. President. That's my birthday kiss from one of the secretaries.' And that will remind the President of my birthday and then he will give me a gift."

I laughed. "That sounds pretty commercial to me, Manolo."

"No, Mr. Atkins. It's not commercial at all. Last year I reminded him that it was my birthday, and he gave me a beautiful, extremely expensive fishing rod. Eventually today he will remember it's my birthday and I will get another present."

Half an hour later a secretary in Ron Ziegler's office came by. "Manolo," she said, "the kiss I put on your cheek is wearing off." And she gave him another.

PART TWO

The White House Years: Tragedy

April 30, 1973   /   Washington, D.C.

This day would be a day of reckoning. In the morning the President was still at Camp David, having gone up Friday night and spent all day Saturday and Sunday there. He would be there most of today too, determining what course to take in connection with the Watergate break-in at Democratic National Headquarters.

Early today, Ron Ziegler announced in the press briefing room that the President had asked for and accepted the resignations of John Dean, counsel to the President; Bob Haldeman, chief of staff of the White House; and John Ehrlichman, head of domestic affairs and special assistant to the President. He had not asked for but had accepted the resignation of Attorney General Richard Kleindienst. And to fill that spot he had immediately appointed Secretary of Defense Elliot Richardson.

The President said he would make a nationwide radio and television address at 9:00 P.M., tonight. I worked around the White House most of the day, where things were strangely silent. Nobody was saying anything. Usually the place is a chatterbox. The seriousness of the Watergate thing had suddenly caught up with everybody. I saw Bebe Rebozo in the West Wing. I imagined the President had asked him to come up to be with him during this trying time.

I quit a little early, came home and ate, and then went back about 7:00 to prepare for the television address. The speech was to be made in the President's office. Al Snyder, the President's television advisor, had set things up on a television-newsreel pool basis.

The President did not come in as usual to check out the lighting or to make a sound-level test. About five minutes of nine, I decided to go down to my office and hear the speech there, then come up immediately afterward to make photographs. Jack Kightlinger was with me—he would do the black and white and I the color.

The President's speech was an emotional one. It lasted for about twenty-five minutes, but when I sensed that it was winding down, I ran upstairs with my camera and stood in the hall outside the President's office, where I could just barely hear his voice. As soon as the telecast was over, I slipped into Tom Hart's office, where the recording people sit, and went to the door that leads into the Oval Office. It is always jammed open by cables. I walked into the President's office but the President wasn't at his desk. He had already finished and was talking to a lighting technician whom he recognized as one of the old faithful press personnel.

What he actually said I don't know, but he was weeping, and he had his hand up up over his eyes. I could see that his eyes were red and he was greatly disturbed. When he went out the side of his office, I assumed he had gone to the residence. But he had not. He went into the press room. Jack Kightlinger was there and he told me that the President had stopped briefly and chatted with members of the press. He told them that the press had been right in pursuing the Watergate thing. He said he was sorry it had happened and that he would make every effort to see that nothing like it would ever happen again. Now, he said, it would all be straightened out.

Then he had broken away from the group and gone up to the second floor of the residence.

Memorial Day Weekend, 1973   /   Key Biscayne, Florida

The President and Mrs. Nixon, Mr. and Mrs. Ed Cox, and Mr. and Mrs. David Eisenhower went to Key Biscayne. It was an unusual occasion, having the whole family in one place at one time. It was decided to go over to the Robert Abplanalp place in the Bahama Islands.

Normally I would have gone with the press pool to Walker Cay, but on this trip I was asked to stay at Grand Cay, where I was told to make some family photographs. I had an idea this was Julie's brainstorm.

As soon as we'd arrived in the afternoon, the family immediately set out to go fishing in Abplanalp's boat. I went aboard a Coast Guard cutter, but the cutter stayed so far away that it was impossible to make any pictures. The few snaps I did take didn't amount to much.

As the Nixon party departed from the dock, I made several shots that I thought might possibly be of interest. That was Saturday night. Sunday evening the whole Nixon clan went swimming in the sea. The area has some very lovely beaches, but also an awful lot of dangerous coral. It is a black-type coral, the sharp edges of which show even in the middle of the beach and which can easily tear a person's skin.

Bebe Rebozo and Bob Abplanalp were planning a lobster cookout on the beach. Well, Manolo Sanchez took a dim view of picnics on the beach. He also took a dim view of the whole Grand Cay eating operation.

(*133*)

Youngsters eagerly grasping the President's hand.

This little girl was ideally located when the President walked over to an airport fence to greet the crowd.

He felt that he could cope better in a kitchen and around a dining room table.

I was quartered in Beach House No. 1 with a military aide, a couple of Secret Service men, and a physician. After I had made snaps of the group in the water, I went back there to await a call to work during the picnic. There was a very black cloud blowing in from the south. I asked Lieutenant Colonel Gene Boyer, the pilot of the Presidential helicopter, about the possibility of rain. Like all fliers, he's a weather-watcher and studies the charts. He said it was a strong possibility that the big thunderheads were going to go right over the island.

By this time Manolo had the potatoes cooking and the water boiling for the beach party. All the dishes and silverware were brought down to the beach cottage where Julie and David were staying. The plan was to sit up on the deck of the beach cottage and eat there. But once the wind started to blow and rain fell, it was decided to call off the beach party and eat in Abplanalp's house.

I never saw Manolo so mad before. He told me in his broken English, which gets even more broken under stress, "This always happen here! I hate this place!"

He had to carry all the cooked lobsters and the potatoes that weren't finished and all the silverware and dishes and everything else back up to the house and start all over again there. While he was doing that, I was told to take some family pictures.

I made some shots of the Nixon clan, with and without Bob Abplanalp and Bebe Rebozo on the deck of the Abplanalp residence. With a beautiful sunset in the background, it would have been a good shot. But there was no sunset; the sky was covered by black thunderheads.

The Nixons eat fairly early, so it was only seven o'clock when I had finished up there.

Gene Boyer had gone to a store and bought a dozen steaks and some potatoes. He cooked them out on one of the gas barbecues. I had a great meal.

June 17, 1973 / Washington, D.C.

General Secretary Leonid Brezhnev arrived this morning for a state visit of approximately ten days. He flew in by helicopter from Camp David, where he had spent the night. From the grassy Ellipse between the White House and the Washington Monument he came in by automobile to the south grounds. The President and Mrs. Nixon were there to greet him when he alighted from the car.

After Brezhnev had gone through the usual drill, he broke away from the President and went over and hit the crowd just like an American politician during a campaign! The crowd that he approached went wild. Unfortunately, no pictures resulted because there were no photographers there. From my vantage point I couldn't get in close. Nor was it even worth trying to get a shot because I couldn't see the action well.

Brezhnev and the President then stood out in front of the crowd clenching hands over their heads, just like the Presidential and Vice-Presidential candidates at a nomination. After going down a line of troops and getting to the other side, they did the same thing. And again Brezhnev broke from the President and hit the crowd for a double whammy.

At the rostrum, where some welcoming remarks were made, Brezhnev spoke in Russian, with instantaneous translation by a very good in-

President Nixon's rather simple chair in the Oval Office.

terpreter. The next destination was the Blue Room. Here the President and Mrs. Nixon, Secretary of State Rogers and Mrs. Rogers, and others lined up in a receiving line to shake hands with the entire official party. It was at the point when the President and Mr. Brezhnev had gone over to the Oval Office that the press was invited to photograph the two leaders. There were so many photographers that we had to run them in four different shifts. I kept looking after my counterpart from the Russian side, and of course I clicked off a couple of shots myself.

Ambassador Anatoly Dobrynin had given me a Russian camera called a Horizant, which makes a long narrow picture. Instead of the shutter opening for the exposure, the lens actually travels across the film to prevent distortion on the sides. Worth about $80 in Moscow and about $250 in the United States, the camera is sold by very few places because it's of the special-purpose variety which the average photographer would have very little use for. But in that sea of photographers, with all those different cameras pointed at him, Brezhnev recognized the Russian camera and pointed at it: "That man has one of our Russian cameras."

Through his interpreter he asked me whether I was happy with it, and I replied that I was very pleased with it and used it quite frequently. From then on Mr. Brezhnev kept his eye on me to see whether I had the Russian camera. I did use it several times, but there's a limit to how many long, narrow shots anyone would want.

In the afternoon we went up to Camp David, where we made various photographs. The President and Brezhnev walking along one of the pathways under a heavy row of trees turned out very well in the lightly overcast day. It's much better to work in the woods on an overcast day than on a sunny day; sunlight gives you too many shadow and highlight areas.

I rushed the film of the Brezhnev visit to the laboratory.

June 18, 1973 / Washington, D.C.

This morning we hung jumbo color photographs in the West Wing of the White House to the amazement of everybody. I sent some 11″ x 14″ prints over to Dick Campbell in Henry Kissinger's office and told him that they should be sent up to Ambassador Dobrynin at the Russian embassy. Later, in the evening, when I saw the Russian ambassador aboard the *Sequoia*, I told him that I had given the pictures to Mr. Kissinger; Dobrynin immediately put the twist on Kissinger for the pictures since they hadn't turned up.

I'd never taken the cruise on the *Sequoia* down the Potomac with the President, and it was really something. Representing the press were just the official Russian photographer and myself.

However, one of the Russian guards was an amateur photographer, and he kept snapping pictures continually. Even though they were strictly amateur shots, the press photographers who were not on the boat got the impression that the Russians had *two* photographers up there while we only had one. To add to the trouble, this one guy had the unfortunate knack of getting in everybody's way. Nobody was happy with him.

I did make several good shots, and while I was at it, they began serving drinks. Brezhnev had ordered some beer, along with all of the Russians. The waiters went down and brought up the beer.

President Nixon looking out of the window in his Oval Office.

Manolo Sanchez watches the Presidential dogs playing on the White House grounds.

Then Brezhnev decided that he would have something different from the vodka and beer he drinks in Russia. He asked for Scotch. The waiters trotted down and got him Scotch. Whereupon all the others started to drink Scotch. Brezhnev then decided he'd have a little bourbon. That set everyone else asking for it too, and the waiters tore down to get bourbon. Soon there were five different kinds of drinks in front of everybody, and the galley had run out of glasses. Besides, there was terrible confusion as to who wanted what. They were just slamming the stuff through, bringing it up, and putting it in front of anyone.

The President called me over and asked me to tell Manolo to speed up the serving. I dutifully went down to tell Manolo. He was all shook up. "I can't get all these drinks up for everyone! Everyone has five drinks now!" I calmed him down, and he promised to get the drinks up there. But he didn't see anything wrong with the way he was doing it and he was not a little unhappy.

After the little cocktail session was over the President, not without some difficulty, herded the Russians downstairs to the dinner table, where they had a very nice dinner. I know it was a good dinner. Bill Golden, the President's military aide, sent a boy up to get me. Bill Golden, Dr. Chet Ward (whose code name by the way is Sharp Fang), Mr. Brezhnev's Russian doctor, and I sat in another room of the galley and had exactly the same meal they were eating up there at the VIP dinner! By the time dinner was over, we had turned around and were heading back to Anacostia, where we all disembarked and the President and Mr. Brezhnev went directly up to Camp David by helicopter.

The rest of us got in cars and went back to the White House.

June 19, 1973   /   Washington, D.C.

At the crack of dawn, I went up to Camp David. I made some photographs, then came back.

I photographed the President presenting Mr. Brezhnev with a sky-blue Chrysler Imperial. It was a production line model that had been modified for certain extra decor. Brezhnev is a car buff and already has several other cars. On our trip to Moscow last year the President had given him a Cadillac.

Tonight there was a reciprocal dinner for President Nixon at the Russian embassy. To the best of my knowledge, this was the first time an American President had set foot inside the Russian embassy in Washington. The official party went there in grand style. But rather than go up in the motorcade, I got there a little earlier to scout out the best places to shoot pictures. I found a second-floor foyer where I could see all incoming guests. I noticed the huge picture of Lenin hanging on the wall by the stairwell.

I waited fifteen or twenty minutes until finally the President arrived with Mrs. Nixon, along with the Russian ambassador and Mr. Brezhnev and other Soviet and American dignitaries.

When the President and Mr. Brezhnev reached the top step, I made a picture of them. Brezhnev was to escort the President to a room where the VIP cocktail party was going to be held. He got about halfway

Bob Hope, ever the golfer, putts on the Oval Office carpet while an admirer looks on.

A long shot gives a more comprehensive view of the EOB office, where Nixon liked to work.

President Nixon listens intently to Henry Kissinger in the famous Lincoln Sitting Room in the White House. This is where the President liked to meet with members of his staff.

President Nixon and Henry Kissinger walking in the lovely Rose Garden.

through the foyer when he broke away and came over to shake my hand and tell me through his interpreter how fine my pictures were. He referred to the pictures I had given Kissinger's office, which had finally arrived at the embassy.

I thanked him kindly for his compliments, all the time keeping one eye on the President, who was standing by himself in the middle of the foyer while this was going on. I didn't want to be in a position of taking the leader of the Soviet government away from the President.

When Mr. Brezhnev went back to take the President to the VIP room, I made a few more pictures at the receiving line. Then I took a couple of shots as dinner was first being served and that was that. I went home a little early that night, leaving the situation in the hands of Jack Kightlinger, who had the night duty.

June 21, 1973   /   San Clemente, California

The President and Mr. Brezhnev had a signing ceremony in the East Room of the White House today, after which they went to Andrews Air Force Base for a flight to San Clemente. During the flight I made pictures of the President and Mr. Brezhnev together in the Presidential compartment.

We flew very low—only about one thousand feet up—when we went over the Grand Canyon so that Brezhnev could see the vast chasm below. His only comment was: "What a waste!" He meant that if it were fertile farmland, it could grow vegetables.

At San Clemente, we went directly to the compound. The President and Brezhnev went to the President's residence via golf carts. Brezhnev stayed in Tricia's room, which is very much a girl's room. It seemed a little incongruous for such a rough-and-tumble man as Brezhnev to be sleeping there. Andrei Gromyko and Dobrynin were headquartered in the cottage that Julie and David used when they stayed at San Clemente.

The President and Mr. Brezhnev had a meeting in the President's study on the second floor, a beautiful little tower room with a wrought-iron staircase going up to it. They were there with an interpreter and Henry Kissinger. That was the first time I had ever seen the President working in shirt sleeves. I made a few shots in black and white because Ziegler told me they wanted them for news releases.

A reception was held for the Russian party at the swimming pool, which had been decorated with a big Mexican hat, loaded with flowers, floating in the middle. It was all very gay, very beautiful, and very much in the California spirit.

After the guests were assembled, the President, Mrs. Nixon, and Brezhnev strolled into the reception area and went immediately to a microphone in the aisle. But as soon as the President and Brezhnev got to the mike, Brezhnev broke away. He ran toward the pool and clowned around, pretending he was going to jump in. Practically anyone else who'd do this would be regarded as an idiot, but with Brezhnev, who resembles a cuddly teddy bear, it was funny.

Then of course he returned to take his place beside the President. After their brief remarks, they formed a receiving line, and all the guests went through the line. With Brezhnev speaking at great length to many of the people, it took a terribly long time.

June 23, 1973 / San Clemente, California

This morning there was a ceremony in front of the President's residence to celebrate the signing of a joint communiqué by the two world leaders. The Soviet official party was lined up on one side of a table that had been set up, and on the other side was the American official party, about twice as big.

Toward the end of the ceremony, Brezhnev asked his Russian group to move in close so that there would be a tighter picture situation. Well, Ambassador Dobrynin, the man closest to him, was a little reluctant to move. So Brezhnev went over, grabbed him by the elbow, and pulled him in. And then he beckoned the American delegation to move in, and they did. Brezhnev automatically seemed to upstage everybody all the time.

Early in the morning movie star Chuck Connors had presented the Soviet leader with a pair of gold-colored Western cowboy pistols. Several times Brezhnev, who was quite a Western film buff, pretended he was pulling the pistols out of his belt to draw. After the ceremony, Brezhnev spotted Connors, and, instead of heading for the helicopter, made a break for the movie actor. Chuck shook hands at first, but that wasn't enough for Brezhnev. He wanted to give him a Russian bear hug. Two or three times he tried, but since Connors is about seven feet tall and Brezhnev is a little on the short side, it didn't work. Then Connors leaned over, and Brezhnev threw his arms around his neck and jumped up in the air. When Connors straightened up, Brezhnev flew up off the ground about two feet. Everybody got a big kick out of this very funny scene.

Brezhnev then boarded the helicopter with the President; they were flying to El Toro Marine Air Base for the final goodbye.

Knowing by now that every time Brezhnev was in front of the cameras he pulled some trick, I expected that there would be a big bear hug with the President in front of the aircraft due to fly him back to Washington. But there wasn't. There was only a routine handshake. Brezhnev then went up to the top of the ramp, waved goodbye to everybody, and walked into the plane. And that was the end of Mr. Brezhnev's visit to the United States.

The Watergate case developed rather slowly, and it wasn't until after his reelection, when President Nixon had won forty-nine of the fifty states, that it became a real political issue.

In spite of all the freedom of movement I had in the White House because of my job, I still have no idea whether the President knew or did not know about any of the shenanigans connected with the Watergate break-in. However, I do know that after the hearings on the Hill started, a great gloom descended on the White House and all of us working in it. Day after day the Committee questioned people who had been dragged down into this thing to become its victims.

The President is going to speak tomorrow about the Watergate situation before national television and hold a major press conference afterward.

He left for Camp David in the afternoon to put the finishing touches on his speech. As the official White House photographer, I did not make a single shot of Mr. Nixon at work on what might prove to be the most important speech of his career. That disturbed me. The President had sealed himself up with a handful of close advisors. I'd put in requests both at Camp David and at the White House to make some sort of a photograph showing him working on this major address, but my requests hadn't even been answered.

Working breakfasts were habitual with Nixon. Here he is joined by Secretary of Defense Melvin Laird, then-House Minority Leader Gerald Ford, House Majority Leader Tip O'Neill, House Speaker Carl Albert, and Bill Timmons, member of the congressional liaison staff.

Looking back on it, I can see that the first indications I had that there were real problems in the White House staff was in the subtle change in the President's relationship with Ron Ziegler.

Ziegler has never bothered much with me, simply because I'm a photographer and photography to the press secretary is a kind of unnecessary evil.

Ironically enough, in the press corps the supporters of the President are the technicians, the sound men, the lighting men, and the cameramen—*not* the reporters. The photographers in many cases despise the reporters and commentators they work with, especially the television cameramen.

Yet Ziegler went out of his way to court reporters; he played tennis with network commentators who the very same night might rip the President's belly open. It wasn't until Ziegler himself was called a "ten-month liar" in connection with Watergate that he separated himself from the highly paid television commentators fattening on the blood of the President.

Dwight Chapin once said that Ron Ziegler was the most insecure man he'd ever known. One time I showed Ziegler about a dozen portraits I had made of the President, and Ziegler could not make up his mind whether he liked them or not. His solution was to throw them all out. When he did pass on a picture of the President to the press, it always looked like the whiskey's ad's "man of distinction"—exactly the wrong kind of image for the President of the United States.

August 15, 1973 / Washington, D.C.

I made a fish-eye view of the President giving the Watergate speech in the Oval Office. There was a lot of secrecy connected with the speech; I didn't really know it was scheduled until this morning.

Jack Kightlinger and I made the pictures together. I went in ahead of time, when the technicians were checking out the lights and voice level, and got a few shots. I left before the President went on the air and watched the speech on television in my office.

Then, just a few seconds before it was over, I went back up into the Oval Office and waited.

The President struck me as looking haggard and tired. The speech itself had been very low key. Afterward, he went directly to his residence in the White House.

On the following day, Thursday, he had no visitors scheduled. And on Friday he had just one appointment at noon. Immediately after that, he was flying down to Key Biscayne.

The President was scheduled to speak to the convention of the Veterans of Foreign Wars today at the Rivergate Convention Center. Naturally, at one of the briefings in the White House press room, Jerry Warren called it the "Watergate Convention Center," to the accompaniment of hoots of laughter from the press corps.

From the airport to Convention Center the President was supposed to drive in his open limousine down Canal Street, the main drag. Substantial crowds were expected everywhere. But at the last minute the motorcade route was canceled; an assassination threat had surfaced just as the President arrived in town. The Secret Service took over and directed him to drive around through back streets instead. The President was naturally irritated.

When he arrived at the Rivergate Convention Center, my car was a good way behind his. The plan was to stop the motorcade, take the roof off the President's car, and let the three convertibles loaded with photographers drive up alongside to take pictures.

Of course, it didn't work out that way. At Convention Center I had to run a full block with all the other photographers to get to where the President was. He was already shaking hands with a few people in the crowd on the Center steps.

Ron Ziegler was four or five feet behind the President, between us, and I was about to follow as the President turned to enter the Center. But just then, the President swung around and in what I thought was a very unusual state of anger directed Ziegler to head off the press and not let them through the doorway. I don't know what his actual words were. I was watching him closely and he seemed to be shouting at Ziegler, holding him by both shoulders. Then he suddenly swung him around and gave him a one-handed but powerful shove in the back.

I did not shoot the scene. My instincts were to raise the camera and bang off a few frames. But at the same moment I knew that the President would see me clearly, and the sight of his own photographer taking a picture of him in a bad mood might double his anger.

It was the first time that I had ever seen the President lose his cool. To me, it was a disturbing thing. There were some television people right behind Ziegler; they caught the action on film.

In Convention Center later, many of the reporters discussed the incident. Some thought the President might be on drugs or might have had too many martinis. There'd been plenty of talk about that lately. Several of them asked me about it. I told them the truth: I had no idea whether he was on drugs or whether he was drinking martinis or anything else. I said it certainly would be unusual for him to be doing either, but I simply didn't know.

Jerry Warren at the press briefing in San Clemente the next day assured the reporters that the President was neither on drugs nor alcohol, but that he was a little uptight in general. One of the sound men later told me that the President's hands trembled during the San Clemente broadcast, which I had noticed myself. And he said his voice had been a little more raspy and broken, and he tended to shout. I had to take the sound man's word on the voice, because he's an expert in that area.

Anyway, Nixon's sudden flare-up at Ziegler was unusual. It gave me something to think about—something not very good.

August 22, 1973 / San Clemente, California

The press conference held today in the compound of the President's residence had been a closely guarded secret. When I drove in this morning, I had not yet been informed about it. Seeing three huge television trailers from NBC in the driveway, I realized that the press conference which had been hinted at was finally on.

Inside I saw the President's new military aide, General Lawson, having breakfast with the President's other physician, Dr. William Lukash, now an admiral. They invited me to join them. Bill Lukash told me that the press conference was scheduled for eleven, but actually might be held as early as ten-thirty.

But shortly after that, Mark Goode and Bill Carruthers, the two White House television consultants, arrived and told me the broadcast wasn't going on the air until eleven-thirty. We discussed the site and all agreed it was technically a disaster area. With the hot sun directly overhead, the lighting on the President would be bad, and with the incidental traffic noise from the freeway a quarter of a mile away, and the ocean wind, and other problems, the sound would be terrible. In addition, the jerry-rigged platform looked like the third-grade May Day production of well-meaning but incompetent mothers.

I was sitting at the reception desk in Building B when Ron Ziegler came by and asked me how the setup looked.

This picture was taken in November 1972 at Camp David. At the time, Alexander Haig was Kissinger's assistant.

"If you want the truth, Ron," I said mildly, "I have some reservations."

He called me into his office. "What reservations?"

"You're going to have the President out there in the bright, glaring sun. His eyes are going to look like a couple of burnt prunes. His nose is going to be sticking out with the worst possible shadows. And the sound is going to be awful."

"Well," he mused, "it's set up for outside and there's nothing you can do about it. What else are you concerned about?"

"If we had it up in the Century Plaza in Los Angeles and announced it a couple of days in advance, we'd have reporters from all over the country coming, instead of that knot of Washington reporters who travel with us. You're going to have about fifty or sixty hard-nosed Nixon-haters sitting out there today, and that's it."

Ziegler shook his head. "We aren't going to do it in Century Plaza."

By now the press was gathering in force at the San Clemente Inn, waiting to be bussed up to the compound.

"One thing you might do," I suggested, "is bring the press in at the last minute rather than the first. The sun is hot out there. If they sit for an hour before the President arrives, they'll be ready to blow up like boiled shrimps."

Ziegler thought about that a minute and then called Ray Zook, who was handling the press bus; he told him to hold them uptown until eleven.

When they finally did come, they only had to sit outside for about a half-hour before the conference began. Not bad, considering.

The press conference itself was a major success, "substance-wise," as Ziegler would say. Pictorially, it was good. The President looked bad standing in the hot sun, trembly and nervous at first, but as things got rolling, he took command of the situation. He answered all the Watergate questions and explained a lot of them effectively. He then announced that Secretary of State William Rogers was leaving the State Department and that Henry Kissinger of the National Security Council would fill the post.

I knew Kissinger would do a good job. In fact, he probably would straighten out the State Department. No one would be able to give Kissinger, the hard taskmaster, a rough time.

But Bill Rogers was a very kind, decent gentleman, and a true friend of the President. After four and a half years of the State Department, I'm sure he'd had a bellyfull and I guess was glad to go. He was returning to private life, to his own law firm. I was going to miss him very much.

August, 1973   /   San Clemente, California

I left the Surf and Sand Motel around 7:00 A.M. and arrived at San Clemente about 7:25. I called Manolo to tell Julie I wanted to talk to her. A half-hour later she was on the phone and I explained that I was anxious to make some portraits of her for an artist who was going to do a piece for the *Saturday Evening Post*.

I said I'd already sent some stock portraits over, but the editor felt that they were dated. Actually, they wanted the material for a story on Julie. She'd just accepted a job as assistant editor of the magazine and would be doing work with the children's magazines that the *Post* published.

"She wants you looking in a certain direction," I told Julie.

"That's no problem," Julie said. "I'm seeing a CBS television crew this afternoon at three for an interview. We can do it afterward."

The interviewer was a well-dressed, worldly, businesslike woman. She had set up the cameras under a little tree out behind Henry Kissinger's office in the compound. There were lights and reflectors and cables—a real Hollywood-type setup—with two cameras on tripods, two sound technicians, and one gripper (a guy who holds lights and reflectors and things) .

After a lot of bland questions to begin with, the interviewer soon got

President Nixon driving the golf cart from the helipad to his San Clemente residence. Friend Bebe Rebozo is in the backseat.

down to the nitty-gritty. I could guess what she was leading up to. Sure enough, she asked Julie:

"When are you expecting?"

Julie said, "You know, that's a personal matter, and I'm not going to discuss it in public."

Then there was some talk about babies and family planning. The CBS girl asked Julie if she liked children, and Julie said that it was another personal thing, which she wasn't going to discuss.

There followed the questions: As the President's daughter, did she get along with the Secret Service well? And how did she like her house over there that Bebe Rebozo had given her?

"Bebe didn't give me that house," Julie corrected. "He bought the house and David and I rent it from him."

"What's the rent?"

Julie answered coolly. "That's another personal matter. I don't think I should say. It's a good substantial rent, but I don't think I should tell people."

"Why not?"

"I don't tell what my college grades were, for example. They were pretty good, but I don't go around bragging about them. I regard them as something personal. Do you understand what I'm getting at?"

"Not really," said the interviewer.

Julie was waiting for the interview to stop, but it didn't. I stayed right there in range so she could raise her eyes to me if she wanted to; I would then call her off the set.

She stuck it out, though. Pretty soon it was all over, and the two of us walked over to the house.

"How did I do?" she wanted to know.

"Remarkably well," I said. "I noticed that she had a steno pad filled with questions. As she went along, she checked them off. It was arranged so she'd lead from bland questions to irritating ones. If it blew up there, the rest of the talk wouldn't go down the drain."

Julie laughed. I remarked that I thought she'd get public sympathy from the show.

When we got over to the residence, the President was sitting in his golf cart, and the limousine was at the front door. Bebe was standing there.

Julie said, "I have an idea that my father wants me to go some place with him. You stay here a minute and let me run up there. I'll give you a signal if you should just go on."

Julie spoke to her father, signaled, and a few minutes later the car passed me. The windows were full of hands waving at me. I waved back.

October 10, 1973   /   Washington, D.C.

This is a day for the history books. The Vice President of the United States, Spiro T. Agnew, resigned after repeatedly affirming that he would never resign under fire.

I was on an errand in Washington buying a couple of ties and had the car radio on when suddenly a call came through a second radio channel: "Hawkeye! You're wanted back at the White House. Emergency. As fast as possible."

I drove back to the White House through terrible traffic. It was so bad that I jumped out of the car two blocks off and ran the rest of the way. Two of my men were outside the President's office, substituting for me.

I went up with two cameras, one black and white and one color. Tom Hart told me that the President had asked for me to record a historic event. "See that Ollie is here to do it," he had told him.

It was one-thirty in the afternoon, the dead part of the day when nothing ever happens. When I walked into the Oval Office, I had Bob Knudsen with me. "This is for the record, Ollie," the President said. Henry Kissinger handed the President a piece of paper and the President was grim and Henry was grim as they both held onto the paper long enough for me to make three or four exposures.

Bob shot black and white and I shot color. The paper was the written resignation of Spiro Agnew as Vice-President of the United States. The mechanics had been performed the day before, and the resignation took effect four minutes before I made the picture, at 2:00 P.M. A good many things in life have startled me, but this was really a shock. Amid all the other crises, criminal complaints, court cases, and charges and counter-charges lately, this was the worst blow of all.

After I had made four or five frames, I said, "Thank you, Mr. President," and Bob Knudsen and I walked out the side door. I went down to the office without saying a word to anyone, unloaded the cameras, and called the laboratory to tell them to send a car immediately to pick up the roll of film. The photos were for the record, not for release, but I've seen signals turn very often and I thought they might again. The historic document I had photographed changing hands was bound to be eventually released to the press.

Immediately after that, the President met with General Haig, and I photographed that. He called in the Republican leaders of Congress—the Senate and the House—and they all grouped around his desk with General Haig in a serious dialogue. I photographed that too.

For the rest of the day I was invited to pop in on every other meeting that took place. I photographed the President with Mel Laird and Bryce Harlow. Then the President invited down the Democratic powers: the speaker of the House, Carl Albert, and the majority leader of the Senate, Mike Mansfield.

General Haig, not sure that he should be at the meeting, asked the President whether he wanted him to attend. "Yes. Please sit down," said the President. While this was going on, I stood behind the President's desk and photographed the President talking to the Democratic leaders.

The conversation concerned what was to be done. It's not my job to report the words, only to photograph the event, and this I had done. I went outside and looked in through the window. There I made additional photographs of the four men seated in the President's office talking about the crucial governmental situation. With the resignation of Vice-President Agnew, by law Carl Albert, speaker of the House, was the successor to the President and had already obtained Secret Service protection.

Earlier in the day the President had invited Republican congressional leaders to the White House to discuss the progress of the Arab-Israeli war. I made some special wide shots with my Russian camera from behind the President, showing the entire group leaning over the big H-shaped table in the Cabinet Room. Photographically, it was a study in concentration.

I had then gone down to the office to wait for the visit of the President of Zaire, the country that used to be the Congo. I had photographed General Joseph D. Mobutu before, when I was in Africa with Stewart Alsop during the Congolese revolution. I remember taking pictures of him in the backyard of the government house area there. On my left, overlooking me, there had been a machine gun nest, and on my right a second machine gun nest. A Congolese trooper had escorted me in with a burp gun. Those were the conditions when I had last photographed him. Now he had changed his name to Mobutu Sese Seko and he was at the White House.

Mobutu, who was trying to get military assistance from the United States, spoke nothing but French, nor did his assistants.

While we were in the President's office, the American press was out in front of the White House, grabbing the congressional leaders leaving the Cabinet Room and asking questions about the Arab-Israeli War. I was the only photographer in with the President. Mobutu looked around curiously, wondering why reporters weren't in the Oval Office. Tom Hart, the President's appointment secretary, explained that the press was delayed, but President Mobutu could not understand why.

I said, "Monsieur le Presidente, le press Americain et le press Afrique ici tout suite pour photographer vous and le President de les Etats Unis." He understood my broken French.

President Nixon turned to me, absolutely staggered that I spoke French. I think it was the first time he'd heard me say anything but "Good morning," or "Good evening."

Then the interpreter finally caught on and translated what I'd said into English. I saw the President sort of nod in my direction as if I had at least been a contributing factor.

The American press never did get in there, but the African press did, six or seven strong. A press photo opportunity was established for the end of the meeting so the Americans could make pictures. We were running an hour late all morning, and I sensed a certain tension in the air, the kind of feeling you get around the White House when things aren't going quite right. But I couldn't sort it out.

Eleven scientific award winners were to be presented with plaques over in the East Room. One of them was of particular interest to me because Fred Eckhardt, one of my friends at the *World Book Encyclopedia,* had requested good coverage of him. While I was standing in the hall waiting to do this, General Haig walked up and said, "Ollie, keep the cameras loaded all day. We are going to be very busy."

General Haig had never spoken to me in this manner before, so I took it very seriously. I found out later of course that General Haig knew about the Vice-President's resignation and was just trying to give me unofficial warning that I should be alert.

November 4, 1973   /   Key Biscayne, Florida

I went down to Key Biscayne for the weekend. Thinking we could get some special shots of the family, Julie encouraged everyone to go. But the closer we got to the day, the more people in the family chickened out, including her mother, Tricia, Ed, David, and Julie herself. It wound up that no one was going down there but the President and me and members of the staff.

When we got there, I had absolutely nothing to do.

Sunday afternoon I had a summons from Bebe Rebozo to call the switchboard immediately. Bebe told me that I had been invited to the President's residence at six for dinner. "Bring your camera," he added. The story of a photographer's life: He's invited to weddings, receptions, sorority teas, and everything else—to take pictures. "Bring your camera."

I walked in just behind several of the guests, having carefully come on time but not early. It was about one minute after six. Had I been a working photographer, I would have been five minutes early, but this time I was a combination guest-photographer.

A U-shaped table was set up around one side of the swimming pool overlooking Biscayne Bay, over which the sun was just setting. This was really my first chance to get a good look at the pool. It had two sections, one with hot water and the other of a normal temperature. The hot part —I think they said it was 140 degrees—was almost a steam bath. I put my hand in and took it right out. The rest of the pool was pretty warm too. The entire pool was covered with structural steel beams that supported mosquito netting so that no bugs, leaves, or vermin could get inside.

The other members of the party were Rose Mary Woods, Dr. Walter Tkach, Mr. and Mrs. Fred Buzhardt, Mr. and Mrs. Pat Buchanan, Ron Ziegler, Bebe Rebozo and his girlfriend, and the President.

Pretty soon Manolo spotted me.

"Come here, Mr. Atkins, come here!" He was motioning me back to the kitchen. Since I was a guest at the President's dinner, I didn't really want to go there.

Pretending I didn't see him, I kept on talking with Bebe and the President. I was waiting for a chance to mention how well Julie was doing at her job with the *Saturday Evening Post,* but it was impossible to get it into the conversation gracefully. I knew the President would be very pleased to hear this report, but I never got a chance to tell him.

I stood around with the rest of them. People kept coming and joining the conversation so that it became one big circle. It was all light talk; no conversation of great import tonight. This being my very first dinner with the President of the United States in a small party at his residence, I was loath to dominate anything. I held myself in the background to study how things were going.

I had set my cameras over to one side. Finally, I decided I'd go over and hook up a flash and get things ready in case I was asked to make a picture. On seeing me, Manolo was so insistent about my going back to the kitchen that I did so. He then slipped out the side door and wasn't there. The Puerto Rican and Filipino waiters, all of whom knew me, thought I was a working stiff and didn't realize I was a guest either.

"Would you like to have this, Mr. Atkins?" they asked, offering me little tidbits of Mexican food, including some guacamole salad on celery.

"I'm a combination guest-and-worker here tonight," I told them. "I think I'd better lay off until I'm at the table." At this, they all looked at me with great awe and said, "Hey, wow, that's fine Mr. Atkins." And that was all.

I went back out. The President, very anxious to get everybody seated, gave some instructions to Bebe, who then told everyone to sit down at the proper place cards. On one side of me was General Haig's daughter, a pleasant teenager, but nobody I could talk to, and on the other side was Mrs. Buzhardt and then Bebe.

Bebe had brought his Polaroid camera. "Ollie," he said finally, "why don't you make a few shots with my Polaroid camera?"

I snapped in a bunch of bulbs and told the seated group, "I'm making a picture of everybody at the table now. This camera has limitations, so I'm going to shoot three at a crack. I'll go all the way around the table."

While I was doing this, Manolo came out, grabbed my chair, and put it under another table as a gag. It was a typical Manolo joke, but I had seen him do it.

After that everything went normally. I must say the Mexican dinner was delicious. When it was over, the President said, "Let's get aboard the chopper and go back to Washington."

I walked out with them to the staff helicopter and got aboard. Within three minutes we were on our way to Homestead Air Force Base, where *Air Force One* was waiting to take us back home.

Walter Tkach was probably as close a friend as I had on the Presidential staff. Cornering him later, I asked, "Walter, do you have any idea who was responsible for my being invited to dinner? Did the President do it or did Ron Ziegler?"

"I think the President himself wanted you, Ollie," Walter said.

I just couldn't quite believe it. I went over to Rose Mary Woods (there is no one in the world more honest than she) and said, "Rose Mary, I know who was responsible for my being there and I want to thank you very much."

She smiled. "You're badly mistaken, Ollie. The President told me to invite you to this dinner."

"Rose Mary," I said, "I couldn't be in better company. These are probably the closest friends I have in the world. I want to thank you very much."

She said, "Don't thank me, Ollie. The President insisted that you be there."

As everybody in the world by now knows, there is an eighteen-minute blank space on the Presidential tapes that were turned over to Judge Sirica's court in connection with the Watergate case.

Rose Mary Woods, who had been given the tapes to transcribe, believed that an eighteen-minute stretch of conversation between the President and Bob Haldeman was accidentally erased when she answered a phone call. That is, she thought that when she had reached back to get the phone, her foot had hit one of the two or three buttons on the pedal controls, thus erasing eighteen minutes of the conversation as she talked on the phone.

There was some question as to whether what had happened was actually an "accident" or whether Rose Mary was guilty of deliberately doing the erasing—or whether it was simply a matter of a blank spot in the tape caused by defective recording during the original taping. In any event, I was assigned today to make photographs for exhibition in the court, showing just what was supposed to have happened. The idea was to get a series of pictures showing how Rose Mary thinks the erasure occurred.

I went up to Rose Mary's office with my camera, wide angle lens, and an open flash bulb strobe. (The flash strobe gives a better flat lighting for the kind of picture preferred in court.) When I got there, I found I

Richard Nixon on a lonely beach near San Clemente.

was not alone. In fact, I was surrounded by a group of people. One was Charles Rhyne, to whom I was introduced; he was Rose Mary's attorney. One of the three or four other people with him was his son; the others were assistants.

For the other side, the prosecution, there was Jill Wine Volner, an arrogant young woman in her early thirties. She too had three or four assistants with her.

There were so many people in the office that everything became pretty confused. It developed that they didn't know what they wanted me to do, and I had no idea what to do either.

Finally, I said, "All right, now. One person at a time, please. Just speak up and tell me what you want me to do. Mr. Rhyne?"

Jill Volner immediately objected to my calling on Rhyne; and had words with him. After a bit of arguing, they struck some sort of compromise. Rhyne would tell me the shots he wanted, and then Jill would tell me the ones she wanted.

With Rose Mary providing the action, I went ahead and took the angles Rhyne wanted, and then Jill Volner told me the ones she wanted. There was doubt in both their minds as to exactly what they were after, it seemed to me.

Nevertheless I made a group of shots according to their instructions, carefully doing one shot at a time. In all I made twenty-two pictures. It was really a rather simple photographic situation, so there was no need to bracket it. (A photographer brackets a shot by taking duplicate pictures at different settings.) I knew that the laboratory was going to be rushing the film out and that the less of it they had to handle the better off they would be.

During the work, sparks flew between Rhyne and Volner. Poor Rose Mary Woods was confused and nervous about it all, but she did the best she could. While we were set up, the phone rang two or three times and she reached over and talked to various people as if nothing at all was going on in the office. I have no idea who the callers were. On her end the remarks were bland and noncommittal.

When I finished making my exposures, I packaged the film and took it down to the lab car, which was outside waiting. Then I called the lab and told them what to expect, and ordered six prints of each frame. No sooner had the car driven away then I got a call to come back to Rose Mary's office. I loaded another roll of film in the same camera and went up again.

A big argument was in progress about dust marks that the pads on the telephone had made on Rose Mary's desk. It seemed that Miss Volner had lifted up the telephone and found them. She called them "suction cup" marks. Whatever they were, they had made dust marks on the desk.

"Can you photograph them?" Miss Volner asked me.

"Under the circumstances," I said, "it would be rather difficult to show them. After all, they're barely visible to the eye. However, I'll give it a try."

By now General Bennett, one of General Haig's assistants, had come over to the desk and was acting as a sort of neutral observer. He picked up the telephone, looked it over, and turned to Miss Volner. "Those aren't suction cups," he said. "They're nothing but little felt pads."

He was right. As a phone slides around on a desk, it will gather up dust and deposit it in one place; then, as it is shifted somewhere else, it'll move the dust there.

But Jill Volner had the unshakable idea that those dust marks were the key to a vital point. The phone had been moved around substantially, and that indicated to her some wrongdoing on Rose Mary Woods' part.

I took two shots of the dust marks. I made one at F-8 and one at F-11 because it was a very difficult photograph: a close-up of two square feet of an area of the desk to show dust. When I left, they were still arguing.

At my office I unloaded the film, called the lab car again, and sent it over. The lab worked until two-thirty in the morning. The film was pretty well exposed and everything turned out all right.

(*177*)

November 8, 1973   /   Washington, D.C.

In the morning, when I got in at seven-thirty, the prints were there. And at eight, after others had shown up, I delivered them to Rose Mary Woods.

At the court hearing that morning, eight of the pictures were introduced as exhibits, immediately making them public property. And, as public property, they were privileged for press use. The court kept one copy, the prosecuting attorney and the defending attorney each kept a copy, leaving three for the press.

At one o'clock I got the word from Bruce Whelihan, who was working the press office, that he needed ten each of the eight frames. I explained that the lab couldn't get them out until about five o'clock.

Bruce groaned. "I've *got* to have them before that! The networks don't even have them."

"I'll do the best I can, Bruce," I said.

Bob Moore had the complete set out at four-fifteen. The pictures were used that night and the next day on television and in newspapers all over the country.

One particular picture, which was to be reprinted many times and was issued to all sorts of people, tells the story best. It shows Rose Mary making a real stretch for the phone, with her foot on the pedal. I imagined then that it would have wide use and regretted that this had happened to Rose Mary Woods, one of the most competent, honest, and dedicated people who ever lived.

Jill Volner, for the prosecutor's office, had begun giving out interviews the minute she left the office. Less than twenty minutes after she got out of the White House, she had leaked the fact that the pictures were taken and even said the photographs were available to the press.

The phone started ringing several minutes after that.

In March 1974, President Nixon, shown with a Secret Service agent and a naval aide, made a surprise stop at a Houston, Texas, drugstore.

We hadn't made a picture of the Cabinet for over two years because they were hardly ever all there at the same time. Since his first term President Nixon had changed the Cabinet personnel, and it now included people whom purists thought shouldn't be considered of Cabinet rank. They were really counselors to the President.

For example, Anne Armstrong, Mel Laird, Bryce Harlow, John Scali, the ambassador to the United Nations, and Roy Ash, director of the budget, were part of the Cabinet. I had been told that there was no legal definition for a member of the President's Cabinet, and so anyone the President said was in the Cabinet was in it. Fishbait Miller, the congressional doorkeeper up on Capitol Hill, disagreed with that, however, and wouldn't set aside seats for the aforementioned five people. But since the President said they were of Cabinet rank, I decided to include them when I was finally told to make the Cabinet picture.

In the morning, the President met in the Cabinet Room with the congressional leadership for a briefing by Henry Kissinger on the Mideast situation, which included the oil crisis and the cease-fire prospects. While they were in there, I slipped into the President's office to put name tags in the protocol order around the President's desk. Immediately following the meeting in the Cabinet Room, the President was scheduled to come into his office and then go into his private room, where he would wait until I had the Cabinet members all set up in their proper places. Then he was to enter, stand in the middle of the group, and we would shoot the scene.

It didn't work out that way.

When the President left the Cabinet Room, he took Russell Long and somebody else with him. Seeing me in his office, he spoke crossly to me for the first time since I've been at the White House. "Get out," he told me.

There were two guys holding lights, and there was Bob Knudsen and Bob Moore—we were all in there. But after he said that, there was nothing for it but to walk out.

We hung around in the hall while he had his meeting with Senator Long. The office had been changed around to shoot the picture, and I'm sure that upset him, too.

Pretty soon Russell Long left and Mell Yates came running toward me from her office. "Ollie," she said, "The President's out of his office. Why don't you go back in there and wind things up?"

So Bob Knudsen and I got all the Cabinet members herded into the President's office at about one minute after ten. This thing was supposed to come off at ten and the President was now in his private office.

Bob Moore was on the little ladder directly behind me; he had the Russian camera. On a smaller ladder right in front of him was Bob Knudsen, shooting the black and white. I was standing directly ahead of him making color. We waited and waited, and there was no President.

I decided I had better say something to hold the group there. "Gentlemen, this is a historic first," I said. "Never before has the Cabinet been photographed in the Oval Office. It's always been done in the Rose Garden or in the Cabinet Room. As soon as the President gets here he will stand right in the middle. I think it'll be fairly painless."

There wasn't much more I could say.

"If it doesn't work," I added, "I won't be around here tomorrow."

There were a few chuckles. We waited ten minutes more. Fifteen minutes. Twenty minutes. They were standing on one foot and then the other.

Suddenly the door opened and in walked the President. I directed him to where I wanted him to stand and then I went back and took my place.

"Let's make a serious shot first," I said. "But not too serious. A little krinkle in the eyes."

They all looked at me and we knocked off a few shots.

"Now it's time to smile," I told them. "I can't tell you anything to smile about, except I understand that there's a favorable editorial in the *New York Times* this morning."

They all laughed and we shot that. Out of the corner of my eye I saw Ron Ziegler standing in the doorway watching. "There's Mr. Ziegler in the door," I said. "He must have something funny to say."

Ziegler said nothing.

They all laughed and I made that shot.

"Let's get the serious shot again, gentlemen," I said. We cranked off a few more shots. "Thank you very kindly," I said finally. "That's it. I appreciate your cooperation."

Thereupon they all left and went into the Cabinet Room. I don't know where the President went.

Since there was a possibility now of a press photo in the Cabinet Room, I told all my guys, "Get in there and shoot that too." I let them go in, but I stayed out.

I checked with Steve Bull to be sure the President wanted a press opportunity in the Cabinet Room, and I heard the President say, "No, we've done enough photography around here, today." Of course, by now all my guys were inside the Cabinet Room. There was no way to get a signal in to them to clear out.

The President went in, took his seat, called the meeting to order, and my guys—not realizing what had gone on outside—made a whole bunch of shots. The press never showed up. After a few frames, Bob Knudsen suspected something and brought the group out with their ladders and cameras and gear.

The press never did get the picture. Jerry Warren was on the phone about two minutes later. "Ollie, push that. Let's get those pictures released to the press."

So we did.

The thing that made the biggest impression on me on this day was the fact that for the first time since I'd been on the White House staff, the President had really spoken in a rather sharp tone of voice to me. I thought about that a little bit, wondering whether Watergate was getting to him.

March 1974 / Washington, D.C.

I picked up Julie at the hospital in Indianapolis after a trip through Huntsville, Alabama, from Key Biscayne, to take her back to Washington.

She was still pretty weak from the effects of an operation performed recently. After a lot of handshaking with the nurses, doctors, and medical attendants who worked at the hospital, we were able to leave.

Going back on *Air Force One,* besides Julie, were David, Mrs. Nixon, the President, and some of the staff. When Julie got back to the White House, they put her to bed to recuperate.

I decided to send two pictures to Julie every day—one in the morning and one in the evening—as kind of get-well gifts.

I searched through my recent stuff and sent a photograph every morning with just a little-bitty note, and the same thing every afternoon. I picked sunset shots, shots of the beach, things like that. The notes said something like: "Hope you're feeling better."

It was a big hit. I could get things to her whereas maybe a hundred people outside had sent telegrams and best wishes that never reached her. My stuff went directly up through the usher's office.

After several days I ran out of pictures and was wondering what else I could do. Then one day right about that time my wife and I were shopping in a local center called Tyson's Corner and passed by a shop that featured imported goods, most of them from Taiwan, Japan, and Hong Kong. They were selling a mechanical electronic singing canary in a little cage. It looked like a real bird. When you pushed a button on the bottom of the cage, a little hearing-aid battery trilled just like a canary.

I bought one and was going to give it to my mother-in-law, but my wife was afraid she wouldn't know how to turn it off and might be bothered by it. So it sat around the house. I couldn't play it in the house because we had a cat named Ajax who would go mad every time I turned the bird on. He would tear around the house and jump up on things trying to attack the fake bird. Even if we put the bird up on top of one of the highest bookcases, Ajax still tried to climb up and kill it.

I brought it to the White House and kept in the office, where I could play it. Once I took it up and showed it to the guys in the press office. Later I walked by Rose Mary Woods' office. That was the time she was feeling a little low about the eighteen minutes of erased tape material and was worrying about the attacks she had been subjected to by the courts and lobby groups after the President.

I went in with my chirping bird. "I bought you a pet," I said, turning it on. She got such a kick out of hearing the bird sing, I couldn't even take it out of the office. I had to leave it with her.

I thought: *I'll send one of those canaries to my ailing friend, Julie.* My wife and I went back to Tyson's Corner and bought one, even though the price had doubled.

Next day I brought it down to the White House. After Mary Matthews, my secretary, had wrapped it up in plain brown paper from the mail room and I had attached a little note to the outside of it, we sent it to Julie via the usher's office.

She got so great a kick out of it that in a short time she had everybody in the White House looking for me. I was in Dave Hoopes' office talking about a personnel problem when a call came through that Julie wanted to talk to me. When I finally got back to her, she told me how much she enjoyed the canary.

"There's one thing, Julie," I said.

"Oh?" She said, puzzled.

"Don't feed it too much."

March 16, 1974   /   Nashville, Tennessee

On this Saturday night we went down to Nashville, Tennessee, where the Grand Ole Opry was moving into a very elegant and elaborate new facility. For years they had worked in an ancient building that was small, not air-conditioned, unheated, and just inadequate in every other way.

The Grand Ole Opry operation had become so affluent that they were able to build the new building for about $16 million. A huge hall, with the latest theatrical equipment in it, it was set up so that all the programs could be taped for television. Besides that, it was air-conditioned, the seats were comfortable, and the balconies were built so people didn't have to strain their necks to see what was going on.

The President and Mrs. Nixon both made an appearance, Mrs. Nixon having just returned from South America. After watching the goings-on for about half an hour, they both went down on the stage, where the President really got into the spirit of things. He was like an old trooper who suddenly finds himself pushed out in front of the public. All the worries of the Presidency and Watergate seemed to evaporate. With the spots on him, he beamed, tried to use a yo-yo in a way which was very funny, and played a few selections on the piano.

The Grand Ole Opry operation was very casual and informal. People moved around; fans came up and took pictures from below the stage. It was all quite loose.

The drummer at the Grand Ole Opry seems puzzled by Richard Nixon's piano technique.

Country music people are members of a special breed who take things as they come and don't seem to have the hang-ups and tantrums that movie production people have. If someone blunders with a name or goes to the wrong mike, they laugh it off and make it all part of the act. Through all of it everyone has a good time.

The President joined right in, and it was a very successful evening for him. I got some good pictures out of it. With all the woes of the Watergate disaster around us, and the talk of impeachment, it was a pleasure to see the President really being admired by the people.

I heard later that the audience was a "Love America" audience from the Bible belt. Although this was said in a snide way, I considered it really a compliment to the people so described. What better credentials could you have for being a citizen of this country?

March 20, 1974 / Washington, D.C.

For five years I had been trying to get some decent photographs of Ron Ziegler with the President. On many occasions Ziegler had forceably brought this fact to my attention, the last time being about three weeks before.

"Ron," I'd said, "I know you well enough to be sure you will never arrange these pictures. I'm going to take the bull by the horns. I'm going to lie in wait outside Steve Bull's office and when you go in to see the President in the morning, I'm going in there with you and make a few shots."

He'd said, "Okay, we'll do it."

Next morning in walked Ron Ziegler. "Ron," I said, intercepting him, "I'm going in with you, old buddy."

"No, no!" he said. "Not this morning, Ollie. Let's do it the first of the week."

I said, "Okay, Ron. The first of the week."

But that day the whole party went to Key Biscayne and none of us got back until Monday. On Monday I knew the President was feeling slightly rested from a rather pleasant weekend in Florida, so I got up early and saw Steve Bull.

"Look," I told him, "we're in need of some pictures of the President and Ron Ziegler. Would you go in and tell the President that I'd like to make those shots today?"

Steve said, "Sure. We'll do it today."

A few minutes later he went into the President's office with some paper work and told the President about the pictures. The President approved.

So when Ziegler came in about nine-fifteen and went through the door, I walked in right after him.

"Sorry," he said over his shoulder. "Not this morning."

On that carpet in the President's office I can be so quiet that the President isn't even aware I'm there. I'm not sure Ziegler knew I was working. I made some photographs with my Leicas, one with a wide-angle lens, and one with a 90 mm. relatively long lens.

As Ziegler was talking to the President, I moved around to different points in the room and made some wide-angle shots. Then I went over to one of the windows and shot across the President's shoulders, looking right at Ziegler. I wanted him to finish the item he was busy with and raise his eyes to look at the President. The first time he looked up, guess what he saw behind the President—Ollie Atkins clicking a camera at him!

The President wasn't the least bit bothered by it, but Ron was. He didn't say anything, though, and I kept shooting. I made about ten frames of them both looking at newspaper clippings. Then Ziegler looked up and waved his arm for me to depart.

I couldn't believe my eyes. After all the times he'd mentioned taking pictures and after all my plotting to do him a favor, he was dismissing me!

I didn't react right away. I put my camera back up and made a shot. He looked at me again; this time he just stopped everything and waved me away. At that point the President saw what was going on and just burst out laughing.

I looked at the President, threw up my hands in disgust, then turned around and walked out of the office.

Steve Bull couldn't believe it, either, and kidded Ron unmercifully when he came out. "Don't you realize the President okayed the pictures?

Don't you know Julie wants them and Ollie needs them and you need them?"

Ron was a little bit chagrined. In any case, what could have been a very profitable picture session turned out to be a disaster. We were left with probably only one or two usable pictures of Ron Ziegler and the President working at the desk.

March 25, 1974 / Washington, D.C.

I saw the results today of a special picture I had made recently from inside Dr. Kissinger's office, looking out on the steps that led to the President's EOB office.

It had been raining very hard a couple of days ago when I had gone into Kissinger's office and shot through the window. The scene showed the structure of the window, the curtains coming down, and a straw magnolia in bloom over on the right side of the steps. There were two lamps on either side along the steps and a railing right down the middle.

The President was coming down one side and Alexander Haig down the other. Manolo was there carrying an umbrella high up, shielding the President a little bit, while Haig walked in the rain. In spite of Manolo's umbrella, the President was getting pretty wet.

It made for a spectacular, different kind of shot. All the time I'd been around here I had never thought of doing this.

In addition, I had planted Jack Kightlinger downstairs so he could take another shot of the President with a different kind of lens from the doorway. In that way, we got two cracks at the picture.

Just before the President came out, Ron Ziegler strolled down the steps by himself, and I shot one of him in the same situation. He happened to look up and, seeing me in the window, grinned and waved. I sent him that picture today.

While I had been lying in wait in Kissinger's office, I'd happened to look around the place. On the south wall there was a huge painting, four by eight feet, in an elaborate frame. This whole canvas was painted blackish purple, and just off the center there was a black dot about the size of a quarter.

And that was all.

I didn't know where it came from, whether it was Kissinger's personally, or whether it belonged to the GSA, which normally supplied the art that was hung around the White House.

I saw Julie, who had requested an appointment with me, at one o'clock.

When I got up there, I found her bottle-feeding a very tiny baby, of two or three months. I had heard the baby crying as I came upstairs to the residence on the third floor, but I thought it belonged to a visitor and paid no attention.

Julie explained that the baby belonged to one of her staff people who, for some reason, couldn't leave the baby home today and so had to bring him to work. That's how Julie had wound up taking care of him.

It was amazing to me that with all the people around here who could take care of a baby, Julie would end up to be the one feeding him.

She was sitting in a chair next to her bed. The telephone, which was on the bed, rang two or three times while we talked. As she was feeding the baby, she was worrying about burping him. I don't know a thing about babies, but I noticed that the bottle was one of those plastic ones with a plastic bag in it.

"I think that's a special bag that doesn't let air in with the milk," I told her. "It collapses as the milk is withdrawn. So it's not necessary to burp him."

"Maybe you're right," she said, "but I think we ought to do it for good measure. He's been crying for a long time, and he's very tired."

Fina Sanchez came in then, right about the time that the baby had drunk almost all the milk in the bottle and was going to sleep in Julie's lap. Julie suggested that Fina change the baby, and Fina took the baby away, the bottle still in his mouth.

Julie had just compiled an anthology of children's stories for *Jack 'n Jill, Child's World,* and some other Curtis Publications periodicals that publish children's stories for the age level of seven to twelve.

She wanted me to make a color picture of her reading to a small child for the book jacket. I'd already found the small child, and we planned to do the picture in a couple of days.

April 18, 1974   /   Washington, D.C.

———————————

Yesterday we got back from Paris, where the President had gone for the memorial services held for President Pompidou. Following the services, the various heads of state requested an audience with the President, and he saw one important person after another. The French press was really rather critical of this activity, but it was a great opportunity for those who wanted to talk to Nixon.

The President was greeted effusively by Prime Minister Kakuei Tanaka of Japan, Presidium President Nikolai V. Podgorny, of the Soviet Union, the presidents of Germany and Italy, as well as a half-dozen other important people.

After working very hard for two days, we took the long flight back. Quite a few good pictures had come out of the trip, and we decided we would hang some of these on the White House press wall. I would also have to prepare pictures for release to the news magazines. In all, it had been a very successful trip.

June 1974 / Egypt

We went on a nine-day Mideastern trip that physically was tougher than the China trip. There were motorcades, dust, dirt, heat, food that you had to be careful about eating, and water that you didn't dare drink.

It was, frankly, a terrible physical hardship on everybody. The President rode for miles and miles in the hot sun and went through an endless round of ceremonies, luncheons, dinners, entertainment.

The first important city on the trip was Cairo, Egypt. At Cairo International Airport the President, Mrs. Nixon, President Sadat, Mrs. Sadat, and other officials, went into the VIP lounge. Here the Egyptian official photographers completely ruined the arrival ceremony by running out three or four feet from the President and taking head shots of him, obscuring him from anyone else. They blocked all news coverage of the ceremonial handshake, the military salute, and other handshaking operations.

I had gone in with them, but it was so dark I couldn't make a picture without a flash. I pretended to, anyway. These guys were absolutely ruthless, jumping all around and banging into people. I stood aside. Looking over at me, the President saw me on the sidelines and nodded slightly, knowing what I was going through.

While I was in the VIP lounge, the photo trucks that were to precede the President on the motorcade into downtown Cairo were forming.

President Nixon with President Sadat in Alexandria, Egypt. At a time when Nixon faced adversity at home, some two million Egyptians gave him a hero's welcome.

The convoy consisted of two pickup trucks, which were loaded so heavily that the fenders were rubbing the tires, and a stake-body truck. When I tried to jump on the tailgate of one of these trucks, my glasses bounced off my head onto the street. I jumped off and picked them up, but of course after that the trucks were half a block down the street and I had to run after them.

Eric Rosenberg, one of the advance guys who worked with the press, ran down and stopped the trucks for me. It was at least 100 degrees, and I was exhausted.

I finally climbed up into the stake-body truck. The motorcade was scheduled as a thirty-minute deal, but it took an hour and a quarter, during which we really got beaten and pounded. I found out later that the trip from the airport to Qubba Palace was over seven miles.

Thousands, maybe a million people, thronged the road and greeted the President with a roar of shouting and clapping. We finally arrived in Cairo at the Qubba Palace, which is located on a 200-acre estate that was once a seraglio for King Farouk.

The truck finally pulled up in a position where we could photograph both Presidents' official statements, which they delivered as they stood at the top of a stairway leading into the Palace. This was staged strictly for the press. At this point I had expected to be surrounded by solid humanity, but there wasn't a soul there except us.

In the morning, the President had a meeting with President Sadat, after which we all went on a three-hour train ride to Alexandria. In the middle of the private train there was a special car with a built-in open area, covered by a canopy roof across the top and protected by a railing on both sides. As the train passed through the various hamlets, villages, towns, and fields, it would slow down from time to time and the two Presidents would come out on the platform and wave to the people.

Three million people were lined up along that railroad track, the estimates said, and I believe them. In fact, I believe there were probably

President Nixon walks with King Faisal (right) on arrival in Saudi Arabia.

more than three million. We'd go through places and all you could see were the heads of the people. The last time President Sadat had made this trip by himself, seventy-two people had been run over by the train. To their knowledge, the Egyptian security people told our Secret Service later, nobody had been run over by the Presidential train this time.

The people were so close that the President couldn't extend his arm when we passed through the crowds. In a few instances when the President's hands did reach out to touch the people, this worried the Secret Service agents very much and they shielded him.

The car platform was crowded with people, too; there were about thirty people out there. They were not all press, but mainly Egyptian security agents and officials.

Although I made a few pictures, it was technically an impossible situation. The President was in a shaded area and outside the umbra, in the light, were five stops' difference because of the bright desert.

When we got to Alexandria, we were transferred to another motorcade. The population of Alexandria is two and a half million, and local authorities said that two million of them had come out on the streets for our motorcade.

They were in every window, on all balconies, and on the roofs. On the streets they were jammed thirty and forty deep. You couldn't see a shoulder—just faces. Some places along the motorcade route they were two hundred and three hundred deep.

We finally got to the palace where the President was to spend the night and where a reciprocal dinner had been scheduled that evening—a dinner the President was giving for Sadat. At the same time the Egyptian government had prepared a buffet supper for the American press.

Before the American press arrived, about forty of the Egyptian press passed through the hall, and when we got there, it looked like the locusts had hit. There wasn't a scrap of food left—not even a piece of watermelon rind.

The American journalist is a long-suffering soul. The reporters just walked out of the place and forgot about it.

Sadat and Nixon had a meeting in Sadat's private residence across the bay from us, and we took a fifteen-minute helicopter ride over to cover it. About seven members of the press went, including Bob Considine.

Our chopper also took the American ambassador to Egypt, and his wife, some Secret Service personnel, and some Walker communications people. When we got there, the Egyptians immediately took over. They didn't want us to hang around the residence area and took us to a building a quarter of a mile away, where they had a buffet set up.

This buffet was different from the other one; it was elaborately set for about a hundred people. The Egyptians didn't really seem anxious for us to partake of the food. Some of the guys went over and put a few things on a plate, but otherwise it didn't look as if the buffet had been touched at all.

When it was about time for the meeting between Sadat and Nixon to break up, I realized we were at least a quarter of a mile away from the helicopter. Since our Secret Service people had a spare car there, I asked them to contact the command post at the Palace to find out whether the meeting was breaking.

Lo and behold, it *was* breaking up.

I started my gang walking back to the chopper in the desert sun. We were stopped here and there by security guards, and every time we'd be stopped, we'd lose time.

The President's chopper went up—we saw it go—and I heard the second chopper's motor revving up exactly as if it were going up, too. When we got it in sight, I couldn't contact it by radio for some reason.

I ran out and held my hand up so that the Secret Service agent who was directing the chopper to leave saw me. The chopper was actually off the ground when I finally was able to attract his attention.

After he had called it back and it had settled on the ground, I herded the pool inside the chopper. Everybody was hot, sticky, perspiring, and exhausted.

I knew the minute we disappeared from there, those guys and all their relatives would come and clean up the remainder of that buffet. It made me mad to think that it was going to the Egyptians rather than to the working press.

Nothing has changed in Egypt since the beginning of the Christian era—or maybe since even before that. Mrs. Nixon's personal secretary told me that the servant who carried her baggage up to the room made a big point of washing his hands in front of the two women to cleanse himself for having touched what they had touched.

Nor would any of the servants shake hands with Mrs. Nixon. To them, a woman is such a low object that an accidental touch might defile them for life.

We were quite comfortable, however. The entire building we were in was air-conditioned and all the windows bolted shut. Coldest of all was the area in which the President and Mrs. Nixon were located; it felt like the inside of a refrigerator. In fact, one night Mrs. Nixon had to call for the President's doctor because she had gotten the chills. The doctor realized that it was so cold in the room that the First Lady was simply freezing.

The staff got some extra blankets to put over her and then had the Secret Service open one of the windows to let in some warm air. There was plenty of that outside, all right. Of course, after all that, Mrs. Nixon didn't get much sleep anyway.

On the trip back to Washington I sat next to Dan Rather and talked to him at some length. Dan was reading a paperback book on the historical background of Israel and the Mideast. As we neared Washington, I overheard him talking to another correspondent in the huddle near me.

"We're coming into the only hostile city of the trip," Dan said with a smile.

It was the truth. Nixon was a hero in Cairo, but at home he had a hostile Congress, a hostile population, and a hostile press.

Richard Nixon hurries up the steps to his office. This was taken during his last week in office.

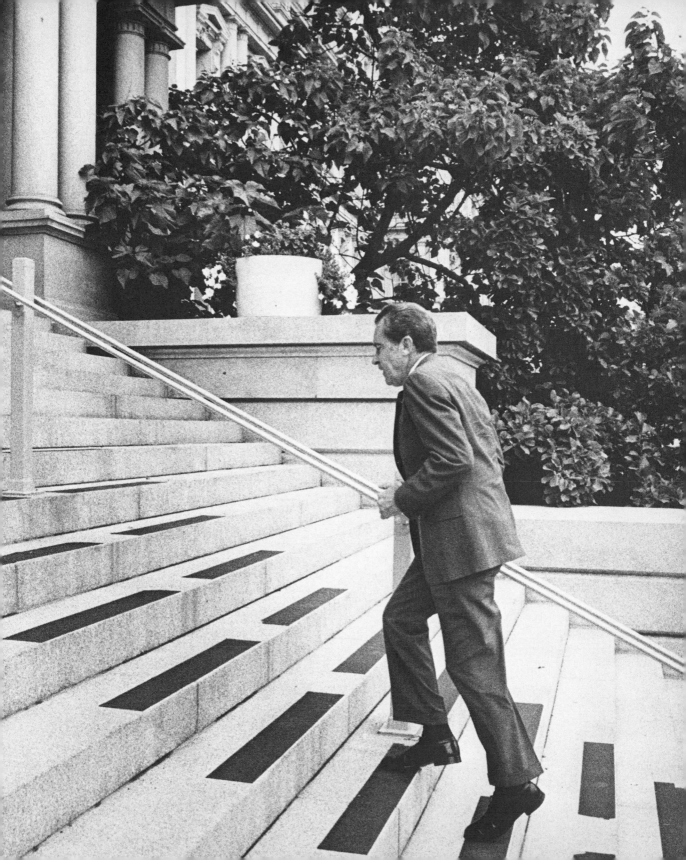

August 6, 1974   /   Washington, D.C.

After the House Judiciary Committee reported out an impeachment bill of President Nixon with three particulars, the bill went to the House, which then considered taking action on the floor by August 19.

Speaker Carl Albert said that the House would expedite its hearings so that they wouldn't drag on; they would be contained within one week, possibly even limited to three days.

The President's situation deteriorated dramatically in the last two days because of the release of new evidence on the office tapes indicating that he actually was aware of and took part in cover-up activities connected with the Watergate break-in.

This was the first time I was touched by the Watergate mess. The tapes mention me very lightly. In several instances the White House staff and the President discussed "Ollie" photos—the ones I made in the President's office when the press was not brought in.

Because the President was in a jam, the press wanted to print proof of this, and this desire increased newspaper demand for more photographs of him.

My assistant Buck May took one call today from a newspaper editor who wanted a "depressing-looking" picture of the President. He came in and asked me what to do about it.

"Tell him we're not giving out any depressing pictures," I snapped.

"Tell him that we have no depressing pictures, that if he would like to have an official picture of the President, we will be glad to send it to him. If he wants to buy that kind of a picture," I added, getting a little mad, "tell him he can probably buy one from the Associated Press. They seem to have a lot of them."

Buck went back and told him exactly that.

The editor said, "Gee, I thought I *was* talking to the Associated Press!"

It wasn't hard to see the thinking that was going on in the press in those days.

August 7, 1974   /   Washington, D.C.

Things weren't really right, with all the rumors and speculations of all kinds, shapes, and sizes that were floating around. Bob Knudsen, who had the day off, called in to tell me he had heard on the radio that the President was going to resign today at four o'clock.

By noon I hadn't seen the President at all, but knew he had been in the Oval Office for a few minutes. From there he went on to the EOB, and that's where he stayed the rest of the day.

I saw his lunch going over about twelve-thirty, carried very carefully on fingertips by a navy steward. Nixon's lunch, which was always covered with a napkin, was reported to be the same lunch every day: cottage cheese and ketchup. I couldn't believe anyone would eat that every day —or even one day, for that matter.

Shortly after noon Senators Barry Goldwater and Hugh Scott showed up with John Rhodes, the minority leader of the House. I didn't know it at the time, but they were bearing a message from the Hill to the President. The drift of that message was, in effect, that the people on the Hill weren't very happy with the administration because of the Watergate revelations and would be much relieved if Mr. Nixon would resign.

Since they had entered the President's office just before I got there, I wasn't able to slip in with them. I waited around outside.

Meanwhile the press had found out about the three of them being

Convened for a final meeting with the President are, from left to right: Speaker of the House Carl Albert, House Minority Leader John Rhodes, Senator Mike Mansfield, Senator James Eastland, and Senate Minority Leader Hugh Scott.

there and had come running in. About two or three hundred reporters swarmed out on the grounds and in the press room. There wasn't a space left to put down a Leica.

After about forty minutes, the President's meeting with Goldwater, Scott, and Rhodes broke up. The door opened and I was standing right there. I made a couple of snapshots through the door, but they weren't good pictures. Knowing this, Barry Goldwater posed himself and the other two for me in the doorway after the door had been shut behind them. I took a couple of shots.

"Now are you really making a picture?" Goldwater asked with that chuckle of his.

I said, "No, sir. I'm making a Hail Mary. I'll say Hail Mary all the way down to the darkroom with this one." Goldwater threw back his head and laughed. "I should have made the pictures in the office, but —the strangest thing—I was out in the hall."

Goldwater, Rhodes, and Scott went out on the north grounds to make a statement to the press. By the time all the cameras had been set up and the television people and the reporters and the sound operators were ready, it looked like the preparation for a Cecil B. De Mille production. In the middle of all this stood a lone microphone and a few clumps of still untrampled grass.

In his statement, Goldwater let the press know, in no uncertain terms, that it had misquoted him in a story.

With my assistant, Bill Fitz-Patrick, I took a few shots of the press conference from fairly high on the steps of a ladder. Then I went back inside the White House and found that the President was in his office. I sensed that I should hang around even though it was getting late in the afternoon and I hadn't eaten. Debating whether or not to walk over to the Black Steer to get a small steak or a hamburger, I heard the hot line ring.

"Ollie," Steve Bull said. "Hang on. You may be doing something up-stairs. Keep your cameras handy."

I sat there for twenty minutes. The television was tuned in without sound and I had the intercom on in my office, listening to the latest gossip from the press room. The Goldwater thing had sort of put the quash on the resignation rumor, according to the press poop.

The phone rang, and the police officer in the basement of the White House came on. "Mr. Atkins, the President wants you to meet him in the Rose Garden. He's coming right down. Wait for him."

"Who's going to be with him?" I wondered. "What am I doing?"

"I don't know, Ollie."

I went quickly to Ron Ziegler's office to find out what this was all about, but I couldn't locate him. No one knew where he was.

I'll just have to go upstairs and face it myself, I thought.

In the Rose Garden I appraised the situation, measured the light, and found the illumination was terrible. It was very harsh, low, western-type light, with the sun at a low angle, a reddish sky, and very, very brilliant light coming so directly at the eyes that everyone would be forced to squint.

But if I shot in the shade, everything in the background would be too overexposed. I had to keep them all in the light.

Pretty soon the President walked out with Tricia, their arms around each other. I started snapping shots.

The President stopped me. "No, Ollie. Don't do it that way. I want you to do it my way. I want a picture like you made during the wedding."

He went over to the edge of the Rose Garden, and he and Tricia walked through the same passage they had used before. I kept shooting in front of them, made about ten or twelve frames, and then backed up a little more and got some of the White House in the background.

After I had enough, I said, "Mr. President, I think I've got it. Thank you very much."

"Ollie," he said, "keep your chin up."

"Mr. President," I assured him, "we've got our chins up. We're all rooting for you, don't worry about us, sir."

He moved away with Tricia.

No sooner had I got to the steps going up to the Cabinet Room than in came Ron Ziegler huffing and puffing.

"Ollie," he cried. "On this picture you're going to do, I want to tell you how to make it."

"Ron," I said gently, "you're too late. I've just finished making it."

He paid no attention to what I said. "I want to tell you how to make it," he repeated.

"You don't understand, Ron. I've just *finished* making it. It's in the camera."

"You've got to do it my way," he insisted, but then what I had been saying finally sank in. "You've done it already?" he said in shock.

I assured him I had.

He blew up then and began bawling me out. I can't even remember the exact words he used. He was simply very upset that I'd gone ahead and done this without him and hadn't done it his way.

I let him rant and rave for a minute until he began to slow down. "Now tell me exactly what you did—everything that happened in the Rose Garden," he urged.

I told him, starting off with the President's call to me, and my search for the press secretary.

"Well," he said finally, "*I'm* supposed to be doing this! The President took over for me, but he got it all fouled up! You haven't done it right."

I looked at him. "I did what the President told me to do. I used my best judgment. I tried to shoot a few candid shots, but he stopped me; I'm not going to argue with that. If you were there, you could have directed it, but you weren't. I looked all over for you. The only ones there were the President, Tricia, and I. I did what had to be done. And you've got no right to tell me I did it wrong."

I had lost my temper and was beginning to shout. Ziegler looked startled. "Don't get sore, Ollie."

But now I was really mad and almost enjoying it. "I'm *plenty* sore! I come up here doing my job and I'm where I'm supposed to be and you run in after it's all over and you tell me you're not happy with what I did."

"You know I've been uptight lately," he said lamely.

I understood that. "You can't redo something that's been done," I said. "I did the best I could."

"Don't get sore at me."

"Ron," I told him, "I've been working with you for five years and I've gotten along in the five years and it's too late to get sore now. Let's forget the whole thing and get the film down to the lab."

All the way over to the press room door he kept apologizing to me, so that at last I said, "Don't apologize any more. Forget it. You're uptight. I'm uptight. I'll get the film down to the lab. That's the important thing."

I knew what Ziegler had wanted. He needed a great mood shot like Kennedy walking on the beach, or something like that. What we had was a picture of the President and his daughter looking at each other with their arms around each other in a terrible lighting situation over which I had no control.

But the possibilities for a mood shot had been zilch. The circumstances for making a long shot of these figures in the distance—a moody character thing showing suffering and love—just hadn't existed.

I ran the film over to the lab and called Billy Shaddocks and Bob Moore at home. They got everybody back in and cranked up the lab to work on the color.

I hadn't been back in the office five minutes before the phone rang and Ziegler wanted to see me again. After loading my camera I went up.

"They're going to have dinner up there tonight, Ollie," he told me right off. "I want you to go up there and make some nice candid shots of them eating. Just click all the pictures you can."

He told me the whole family would be there in the California Room, or Solarium as it's also called: the President, the First Lady, Tricia and Ed, Julie and David, and Rose Mary Woods. Knowing enough not to barge right in and try to take pictures of the President at dinner on what might be one of his last nights at the White House, I went to the usher's office.

Shortly before resigning, the President suggested I shoot a family picture. He urged everyone to smile, but Julie had trouble smiling through her tears.

"I'm supposed to go up and make some shots of the President's family having dinner. What's the situation?"

The usher said, "They're going to eat at seven or so."

I waited around until about two minutes to seven. It was true. They were all in the Solarium, ready to eat their supper on TV trays.

At two minutes to the hour I got on the elevator and went up with one of the President's butlers. Normally, he would have gone with me, knocked on the door, and introduced me.

But this time he wasn't quite so brave. "What shall I tell him, Ollie?"

"Just tell him Mr. Atkins is here."

The butler hedged. "Does the President know you're coming?"

"I don't think he does," I admitted. "Ron Ziegler sent me over."

He looked at me. "I'll open the door and just tell him you're here."

I nodded, but when he opened the door, he was afraid to poke his head inside. Looking past him, I could see the whole Nixon family and Rose Mary Woods seated about in the wicker furniture the room was furnished in. The women were all teary-eyed, particularly Rose Mary Woods and Julie. You could see the tears.

David Eisenhower and Ed Cox were in their shirt sleeves and looked glum and subdued. The President, as always dressed in his business suit, was over in the corner talking softly to Julie.

When I stepped in the doorway, I must have broken some sort of spell, because they all turned around and gave me a warm, joyous greeting.

"Ollie! Come on in!"

Inside, the first thing that happened was that Vicki, the little French poodle, ran up and started to bark at me.

Mrs. Nixon came up and grabbed me by both hands.

I said, "Mrs. Nixon, I'm over here to make informal pictures of you all having dinner." It was a pretty dumb thing to say, because it was so obvious what I was there for, with the cameras hanging around my neck. "I understand you're going to eat on trays."

"Well, I don't really think we're going to eat at all," she said slowly. "I haven't given it a first thought."

"A picture of the whole family eating would be pretty good," I suggested.

"I don't even know *when* we're going to eat. We're just sitting here talking about—things. It's so good to be all together, we're not even thinking about eating."

I didn't know what to say.

"You're here," she went on, "but we don't want any pictures, Ollie. You stay."

The President disengaged himself from Julie and came over. "No. Let Ollie make some pictures. In fact," he brightened, "let's make a family picture."

It wasn't what Ziegler wanted, but I nodded anyway. "I'll be glad to do that."

He started organizing his usual group picture, and before I could make any informal snaps, he had them all lined up: he and Mrs. Nixon in the middle, the Coxes on his right, and the Eisenhowers on his left. Rose Mary Woods was behind me, watching.

Julie, who had been crying, was having a lot of trouble trying to wipe away the tears. Her eyes were red and her cheeks were wet. Tricia, who had been crying too, was dry-eyed now, and Mrs. Nixon was cool and steely calm as usual. Both the young men were able to smile by now.

It was a pathetic thing and brought tears to my own eyes, just watching them.

A lot of animated discussion followed on how they were going to pose for me. Tricia said that she thought the best family picture they had ever made was the time they had their arms linked together.

"We can do that same thing again," the President said, urging them to smile into the camera.

I banged away about six or eight frames of them with their arms locked together. Then when I had the family shot, the group broke up. Turning away, out of the corner of my eye I saw the President reach over and hug Julie very close to him. I made a couple shots of that. It was strictly unstaged, what we call a grab shot.

Then, impulsively, Julie came over and hugged me, and I got des-

A heartfelt embrace from Julie.

perate. Julie's my favorite and I wondered if I was going to go to pieces myself.

Rose Mary Woods suggested that the President be in a picture with the dog at his feet. She coaxed the dog to sit up on the hassock, and the President sat back in his chaise longue with his feet up on the hassock. He actually folded his hands in front of him and *smiled* at the camera!

Next, Rose Mary ran over and kneeled by the President's chair, and I took that. I did all the family shots I could, realizing that I had a fantastic historical treasure on this roll of film.

Mrs. Nixon said, "Now, Ollie, you know these pictures are strictly for us. We don't want you to release them to anybody."

I said, "Mrs. Nixon, I'll do whatever you say."

The President intervened. "No, Ollie. You look through them. You pick out the picture you like best of the family and release that to the wire services. That's your job."

"Yes, sir, Mr. President," I said. "Is there anything else I can do?"

No one had any bright ideas, and so I wished them all a pleasant evening, under the circumstances, and backed out the door.

Trotting down with the film, I saw Jerry Warren in the hall and told him approximately what I had.

"Tell Ron he's not going to get a lot of candid shots of a dinner party. But I've got some good family stuff."

He said he'd tell him.

I had the lab run the car up to grab the film. As I'd expected, the phone rang and it was Ziegler. "I talked to Jerry," he said plaintively, "and I can't make head or tail out of it. What did you *really* shoot?"

I explained patiently what there was and he groaned, "Oh, my gosh, that's exactly what we *don't* want."

"Ron, you're going to get what I took," I said flatly, my patience about at an end. I refused to get into another battle royal.

After a pause, he said, "When can I see the stuff?"

"The color you won't see until ten. The black and white you'll see in about an hour and ten minutes."

"Rush it to me as fast as you can," he said and hung up.

The President with Rose Mary Woods.

Now I could go over to the Black Steer and have my steak sandwich. About nine-thirty I ran the pictures up to Ron Ziegler. He looked at them, sighed, and shook his head.

"Ollie, there's not a single picture here that I want."

"You have got what happened in front of my camera," I said. "Sure, the whole thing was contrived, set up. I wasn't allowed to sleuth around and make candid pictures of a TV dinner. You're lucky they're releasing them at all. I have direct orders from the President that if the family picture is worth releasing in my judgment, it's to be released."

"But *I'm* the judge of that," he protested.

"I'm turning the pictures over to you, Ron, and you make your own judgment. It's okay with me."

He threw them all in the trashcan. Not one picture was selected.

"Ollie," he told me, "tomorrow you and I are going to work together and make some great pictures."

I said, "Ron, I'll be glad to work with you. However, you just threw a great picture in the trashcan. Furthermore, you disobeyed the orders of the President."

"You're still mad at me, aren't you?" he observed with sorrow.

"No, I'm not mad. I'm speaking as a professional photographer."

"Tomorrow morning be your professional best, and we're going to work together and make some big pictures."

I said, "Okay, Ron, I'll work with you tomorrow."

My pictures sat in the trash can in Ron Ziegler's office as I reflected on what I had done today, and how I would explain it to the First Family. The pictures I had made on one of the most crucial days of the Presidency, pictures that were absolutely exclusive, had been chucked in with the trash. It was a difficult situation.

The family picture would have been given a big ride in the papers. I thought it a crying shame that it wasn't going to be released to the press.

Back in my office, I sorted out all the stuff that was down there and reloaded the cameras. It was ten-thirty. I went out, got in my car, and drove home.

It's amazing how absolutely frustrating a job can be sometimes.

Gerald Ford waiting to see the President not long before the resignation.

August 8, 1974   /   Washington, D.C.

Today President Nixon resigned his office as President of the United States, effective at noon the next day. When I got to the office about ten minutes after seven, I found Buck May already there, reading the newspaper.

At the White House mess I had a tall glass of orange juice with a lot of ice in it, a cup of coffee, and a piece of Danish pastry. I was the first one there, sitting in the chairman's seat, but the table filled up pretty quickly. There were a lot of miscellaneous cracks about people over in the Vice-President's staff, and we all enjoyed a laugh or two.

Then I went back to the office. The night before Ron Ziegler had told me that today I would take the most historic pictures of my career, and I took him at his word. He told me to shoot them all in black and white because there would be a lot of newspaper call for them. Furthermore, I would be the only photographer allowed to move close in to the President.

Mr. O'Hare and Mr. Pearce in the usher's office promised to tell me as soon as the President was up. I figured I'd have about seven minutes from that time to get outside to follow him to his office.

After loading two cameras with black and white, I went up to check the existing light; it turned out to be heavily overcast. Then I scouted two likely sites—one by the Rose Garden and one on the approach to

Richard Nixon and Vice-President Ford discuss the departure ceremonies.

This was to be Richard Nixon's last lunch at the White House.

Presidential speech writer, Ray Price, working on the resignation speech.

President Nixon delivers his resignation speech.

the President's office in the colonnade. I marked my spots, measured the light and the focus, and then went back to the basement.

About eight-fourteen the phone rang, and I was told the President was up. I went down to the Rose Garden and as I was checking the light again, saw Manolo Sanchez stride across the walk. He usually precedes the President by about one minute.

"Is he behind you, Manolo?" I asked him.

"Yes. He's coming along very shortly, Mr. Atkins."

Suddenly I saw a figure coming down the colonnade. I put my camera up and was tracking the figure in the ground glass when I discovered it was a Secret Service man going off duty. This was the end of his rotation, what they call a "push." He was coming down to the rest area.

About a minute later the President, looking very businesslike and solemn, came through. I waited until he had gotten to the spot I'd picked out, I clicked off one frame, and wound the camera quickly. Turning, he went through the hedgeway, which I had picked as a spot. I made one frame there, then ran to the other end of the colonnade on the other side of his office.

I had just got one frame there when the President paused and reached up to pull a twig off one of the plants next to the pathway. His arm was in the way of his face, so I couldn't shoot, but what struck me was that I had never seen him do that before. I waited till he put his hand down and then shot one more frame before he ducked into the office.

After running back down to the basement, I sent the stuff over to the lab and told them to print every frame fast. Then, with the reloaded camera I trotted up and stood outside Steve Bull's office, as arranged previously with Ron Ziegler.

I saw Steve. "Here I am," I announced.

"Check, Ollie. I know all about it. Stand by."

Alexander Haig went in to see the President. Then Ziegler appeared and went in. About twenty minutes to ten Ziegler came out, walking right by me, just looking at me without saying anything.

Two minutes later he sent for me. "Ollie," he told me in his office, "the Vice-President and the President are going to have a conference at eleven. It'll be in the Oval Office. These will be some of the most important pictures you'll ever make in your life."

"I understand, Ron."

Outside I told Steve Bull that I was going to follow the Vice-President into the office when he came. I then made arrangements with one of the Filipino waiters to snap on the photo lights when I held up my thumb in a signal.

At two minutes after eleven Vice-President Gerald Ford came in and sat down in Steve Bull's reception area. I clicked off a couple shots of him sitting there.

When Ford got up to enter the Oval Office, I moved in right behind him and gave the signal. The lights brightened as I walked over the threshold into the President's office.

The two men shook hands and then the President turned to me. "Ollie, how do you want us?"

I looked around. President Nixon was always a clean-desk man, so there was never a lot of junk there. But I could see the ever-present cup of coffee, half-drunk, in front of him.

"Sir," I told him, "the light is much better over on the left side of the desk. Let's do it there."

"Sure," said the President, bringing Mr. Ford over with him.

When the two men were in place there, the light was balanced equally between them. I backed up against the bulletproof glass in the President's window and made three or four shots of them. In the first, the President was smiling. I really didn't want him smiling, however.

"Mr. President, let's have a serious talk."

He reacted instantly, and so did Ford. Serious talk began. I don't have any idea what they were saying, but I clicked off three or four shots.

Then I went around to the other side of the desk, where I made a couple more shots. Finally, I went in behind Ford to shoot a picture that was a study of intense concentration, showing President Nixon addressing himself to the Vice-President.

The East Room of the White House, where Richard Nixon made his final remarks.

With that I silently walked out of the office through Steve Bull's door-way, closing the door quietly behind me.

I sent the stuff immediately to the lab, reloaded, and hurried up to Steve Bull's area.

"We want to get one picture of you photographing the President," Steve told me.

I called down to Carl Schumacher, telling him to bring a wide-angle lens and black and white film. He came up immediately.

The Vice-President was in with the President for about an hour and twenty minutes. About twelve-thirty, when he left, Steve Bull went in and told the President that we were waiting. Once inside, Carl went in behind me and while I took a picture of Steve Bull talking to the President, Carl shot me photographing the scene. Unfortunately a waiter clearing coffee cups off the desk got in the picture, and so there was only one frame that turned out to be usable.

I had wanted to get the President standing in one of the windows, so that I could photograph him there, but it never worked out that way.

Shortly after we had cleared out, the President came out and went over to the EOB office. Rushing through the West Wing entrance down the side steps, I beat him over there and made quite a few shots of him trotting hurriedly up the long, almost triple stairway.

He saw me and nodded, alert and smiling. Imagine that—alert and smiling!

I knocked off three or four frames of him on the big stairway. Once he had entered the office, I took up my vigil outside.

General Haig had been chief of staff since Haldeman's resignation. When he showed up, I said, "Al, I really don't have a good picture of you with the President."

He only smiled and walked into the office.

Ron Ziegler came over with Fred Buzhardt, the President's lawyer. I looked at Ron to see if he was going to invite me in, but he didn't. So I cooled my heels again after they had entered.

I never did get asked in, but I was afraid to leave; so I sat there. Ziegler left. Buzhardt and Haig left. Other people came in and went. For me, it was a bad scene all the way.

And suddenly I realized I was starving. I hadn't eaten since breakfast —and I'd had a small meal then. I dialed my office from a little side room off the reception area and asked Carl Schumacher to grab a club sandwich in the White House mess, put it in a doggie bag, and bring it over.

He brought me two club sandwiches, which the Secret Service man inspected carefully before he let him in with them.

Manolo Sanchez joined me and we passed the time of day together. He was reminiscing about his life in Spanish Harlem and such things. When he gets worked up, he keeps lapsing into Spanish, and nobody knows what he's talking about. I just nodded my head and listened, while he kept on going in a marathon English-Spanish talking jag.

The President's lunch had been brought to him on a tray shortly before noon, and it was still in there. I wondered when he would eat it. Earlier, Bob Knudsen had shot the President's lunch as it came over. When the contacts arrived, I examined them. The President had ordered a glass of milk and a section of pineapple with a scoop of cottage cheese on it. So much for the cottage cheese and ketchup myth.

Manolo went inside and then came back out. "Forget about the lunch," he said. "He's not going to eat it. He's asleep."

I jumped up. "He's asleep?"

"Yes. He's taking a nap on the couch."

"What am I doing sitting here?" I muttered. "I've got a millon things to do!"

I went over to the President's receptionist in the EOB office. "Please call me if the President wants me, or if Ziegler wants me."

Then I went down to the basement, where about fifty telephone messages were piled up, waiting for me. They were all from friends of mine in the press corps, and I knew what they wanted. They wanted pictures and the story of what had happened in the First Family's room last night.

I couldn't give them pictures and I couldn't tell them what had happened, so I ignored the calls. There was plenty of work to do anyway. All kinds of prints were rolling back from the lab, with most of the stuff turning out fine: good sharp negatives and everything in place.

When I took them up to Ziegler, he was delighted with them, apparently having forgotten our shouting match of the night before. In fact, he was so darned sweet it was almost sinful, and I was a little suspicious of him. I had never seen him so nice in my life. Maybe I should have blown up at him five and a half years ago.

"Ollie," he told me, "here's what we're going to do now. We're going to release just two pictures to Associated Press and United Press International."

"What about all the magazines and everybody else who's been hollering and screeching?"

"Those magazines have been chopping us up for five years and they can buy them from AP and UPI."

"It's okay with me," I said. "I'm all for it."

"Ollie, you're going to carry the ball on this whole story."

"What story?"

"The story of what happened with the First Family last night."

"Okay, Ron. How do I do it?"

"Frank Ramos has talked to the First Family, and he's typed up some notes about the session. I want you to talk to Frank and go over the notes. Then I want you to give these pictures to AP and UPI and tell them exactly how you made them."

He handed me most of the shots I had taken the night before and that he had dumped in the wastebasket. Among them were the afternoon pictures, too.

I nodded. It was an important assignment, but nothing I couldn't handle.

"Don't hand the pictures out," he cautioned me. "Make them ask you for them."

"No problem."

A close-up of the President and his family in the East Room.

I went down to my office with Frank Ramos, whom I had never officially met before, and we sat down so I could look over his notes.

"You got it right," I told him.

He was a very reasonable, nice guy. He left the notes with me and then went out.

I could hear someone in the hall. I knew that the Secret Service had been told to seal off the White House corridors because the President didn't want to have to speak to anyone; to see tears, or anything else. He wanted the residence clear, and that meant clear of everybody.

The Secret Service agents were locking the doors as they came down the corridor.

I called over to the EOB and asked "Where's the President?"

"He's here, but he's getting ready to leave."

Grabbing the two envelopes of pictures we were releasing to the wire services, I went barreling out into the hall. A White House cop stood at the end of the corridor.

"Where are you going?"

"I'm getting out of here," I told him.

Since all he wanted was to clear the halls, he let me go through the corridor ahead, which led to the press area.

But I didn't want to appear in the press room. I had all those calls from my friends in the business—friends from a long time back—and I simply couldn't talk to any of them until I got the pictures off my chest.

With me I had the shots for release and the two envelopes of the two sets. I couldn't go to the press room and show my face there. So I phoned one of the girls to call Helen Thomas of United Press International and Frank Cormier of Associated Press and have them go to Tom Decatur's office, where I'd meet them.

Hiding in the hallway outside, I waited until I saw them go into Tom's office. Then I walked into the room and shut the door behind me.

Helen and Frank knew what was in the envelopes, but I told them anyway.

"Off the record, I'm telling you that these pictures are being released to the two wire services only. Nobody else is going to get them. It's an exclusive."

Then I told them about each shot and how I'd made it, pretty much as I described earlier. Helen and Frank asked a few questions, but mostly they just took notes.

I didn't return to the office in time to get Ron Ziegler's call that the Cabinet was meeting with the President in the Oval Office.

"Shall I go in and take them now?" I asked when I was in touch with him.

But Ziegler decided that we wouldn't take any pictures, so I didn't. However, I loaded up my cameras and got ready to photograph the President's resignation speech, which was going out over nationwide television and radio from the Oval Office later that day.

Ziegler told me the President wanted absolutely nothing to distract him. The only people allowed in the room would be the technicians actually involved in running the television cameras and the sound, plus the one Secret Service agent who had to be with him at all times.

Most of the pictures I was used to taking of the President making a speech were during "voice-level check," just before the speech began. But in this case, knowing that this was an extremely important speech, I intended to hide behind the television camera and shoot pictures during the speech and risk the consequences.

When Nixon came in, he sat behind his desk, checking the lights to see if any were shining in his eyes or reflecting off the papers. Then he made his voice-level check. I moved out close, shot a couple of frames at the desk, then made two from the side which showed the dramatic atmosphere of the Oval Office with the cameras packed in it.

As I was moving back in behind the television camera, the President spotted me.

"Did you get enough pictures, Ollie?" he asked me cordially.

"Mr. President, I'm going to make a long shot from behind this television camera."

"You know only the CBS crewmen are going to be in this room during the broadcast," he said, obviously guessing what I had in mind.

"I was going to make a shot from this background," I said lamely.

Abruptly he said, "No, no. No more pictures." Then he blinked and looked up again. "All right," he said. "Go ahead. Make another one back there, and you can use it as the official broadcast picture. Take it right now. Then get out."

I did so, making three more shots, showing the television cameras in the foreground. Then I left. Five seconds before air time I slipped out of the Oval Office through the regular door that was now propped open several inches wide with the fat television cables operating the cameras.

I went around to the side of the building to make a shot from the porch area, looking in through the window. At that point, the President was actually making his speech. He never knew I made the shot. Photographically, it's not the world's best picture, but it is a factual record of him as he actually was giving his history-making resignation speech.

On terminating the speech, the President walked right out and went directly to the residence. There were no more pictures for me. That ended my day.

I had no idea how many of the pictures would be used, but I supposed the material would get big coverage.

The next day's events up to the swearing-in of the Vice-President as President would be heavy news. Already the television shows were using the material I had given to AP and UPI. When Ziegler saw some of the stuff on one of the shows, he called me on the phone. He seemed happy about it.

"What I heard on the news was very good, Ollie," he said. "You handled it well."

"Ron," I said, "I was just being honest."

The departure. Mrs. Nixon kisses Betty Ford goodbye before boarding the Presidential helicopter.

Richard Nixon shakes hands with the pilot.

The night before I'd asked Ron Ziegler what he wanted me to do today.

"We'd like you to come to San Clemente with us, Ollie," he said.

So, before leaving yesterday, I'd booked myself on the helicopter leaving the White House and on *Air Force One*.

When I got in in the morning, I found I'd missed one important meeting, but I hadn't known a thing about it. This was the President's staff meeting upstairs in the White House, which was actually attended by only a trusted few. None of them had known about the meeting in advance, either.

The first thing on the schedule was the President's farewell appearance in the East Room, where he was to make his departure speech on live television. I was waiting there when he came down.

By the time he arrived, the place was jammed with White House people—secretaries, staff members, reporters, and television technicians. I assigned my assistants the job of photographing the event, because I had to be ready to leave with the President's immediate staff.

During his farewell talk he was surrounded by his family. At the end of it, when he made a thumbs-up signal, he looked remarkably like he did when he was on the campaign trail. Everybody else was fighting back tears and trying to keep from breaking down.

I got away just before he finished and climbed on board the helicopter. A red carpet extended all the way down from the White House steps to the ramp coming up to the helicopter. As the Presidential group approached the chopper, I made several shots through the hatchway.

I remember that Mrs. Nixon kissed Mrs. Ford, with Tricia and Ed Cox standing in the background and Julie and David Eisenhower beside them.

On the steps of the helicopter the President—he would still be President until noon—gave a V-for-victory sign and grinned out at the crowd. Then he came inside, the hatch closed, and we took off. We choppered over to Andrews Air Force Base, where we boarded *Air Force One*, and then took off for El Toro Marine Air Base in California near San Clemente.

The trip was almost uneventful. The group aboard the plane was understandably subdued and very quiet, although the President did make one stroll back through the aircraft, shaking hands with everybody aboard and saying a few words here and there.

After that, he went back to his quarters at the front of the ship and we didn't see him again until the aircraft landed at El Toro. I decided not to make any pictures of him on the flight. It was untrue, as was reported in the press, that I made some pictures but they didn't come out. You get rumors like that all the time.

Just before we landed, Ron Ziegler told me that the President would pose with the crew of *Air Force One* at the bottom of the ramp after the flight. I got out and made several frames of the President—or former President as he was by that time—with the crew and alone with the pilot.

After the pictures had been made, Mr. Nixon and Mrs. Nixon walked over to their own helicopter, which would fly them directly to La Casa Pacifica. A huge crowd had assembled at El Toro to see the ex-President, and he turned several times to wave at his well-wishers. After he and his wife had climbed up to get into the helicopter, he turned again to wave at the crowd.

I made one picture of him standing there, waving, and that was the last picture I took of him. With his family he was now finally on his

(*240*)

Just before departing: a V-for-victory sign for the crowd.

way to San Clemente, where he would go into seclusion with them for the rest of the day.

It is the custom for the traveling staff of the White House to have some sort of automobile for transportation, especially in California, where everything is so spread out. I had access to a government car, but it took me two hours to get away from El Toro because of the enormous crowd. Traffic was blocked for miles and all the surrounding roads were impassable.

At last, I arrived at Laguna, where I had made a reservation at the Surf and Sand Motel, the normal press residence during the President's visits to San Clemente. It's a very lovely, plush motel right on the beach.

When I'd checked in and got myself squared away, the manager, seeing that I was looking a little bit bedraggled, sent me a club sandwich with a couple glasses of iced tea. I was grateful, because I didn't have the heart to go out to a restaurant to eat after all the emotional let-down of the resignation.

I tried to track down Ron Ziegler and, after a while, finally located him, his assistant, and a couple of the secretaries in a room in the motel. I decided to go over and join them.

"What are your plans for me?" I asked Ziegler.

"I don't know, Ollie," he said. "Just hang in here for a couple of days and we'll sort of see how things work out."

With the President's resignation, a problem had been created with the staff. All staff people were still on the payroll, for the moment, but, of course, everything would change when the new President began rearranging the staff.

Back in my room I found that I had a telephone message from former Governor Scranton at the White House, but when I put the return call through, I learned he'd departed for the day. The Governor had been put in charge of phasing out Nixon's staff and helping Ford put together a new one.

And so ended my last day as Richard M. Nixon's official photographer.

The Nixon family, bound for San Clemente, after leaving Air Force One.

The call from Scranton was a request for me to continue to manage the White House photography office, but not to be President Ford's official photographer. That job had been given to David Kennerly. I flew back to Washington to discuss the situation with Kennerly, who told me he only wanted to shoot pictures and didn't want to get involved with the business operations of the photography office. After working for a few days, though, I discovered we were beginning to get on each other's nerves.

Frankly, my heart was no longer in the work, even though I would have done a good job for President Ford. I felt like a stranger in his group, so after a bit I decided to call it quits.

The changeover begins.